mac's year

1998

Cartoons from the *Daily Mail*

Stan McMurtry **mac**
Edited by Mark Bryant

ORION

For Lizzie

Orion Books
A Division of the Orion Publishing Group Ltd
Orion House
5 Upper St Martin's Lane
London WC2H 9EA

First published by Orion 1998

ISBN 0 75281 739 6

Printed and bound in Great Britain by
The Guernsey Press Limited

An 11-year-old boy from Sharnbrook, Bedfordshire, looked likely to become Britain's youngest ever father after making a neighbour's 15-year-old daughter pregnant.

'The father-to-be says he hopes it's not a soppy girl and if it's a boy it's not going to play with his toys, so there!' *19 August 1997*

Deputy Prime Minister John Prescott unveiled his plans for an integrated transport policy aimed at encouraging the use of public transport systems.

'Tought I's give this public transport thing a try. Tell the chauffer chappie to drop me off at my club, hang about, then pick me up again about six...' *22 August*

Despite a poor turnout at the polls, the people of Wales voted by a narrow margin for a 60-member assembly in Cardiff to take over many of the responsibilities of the Welsh Office.

'Listen, boyo. It's been a while since I was down in the village, but if that Harold Wilson wants a new assembly hall, what's wrong with the old Scout hut behind the post office?' *18 September*

Japanese geneticist Kazufumi Goto planned to use sperm from a 10,000-year-old frozen woolly mammoth to fertilize an elephant and bring the extinct species back to life.

'...Then just before she was born we heard there had been a mix-up at the sperm bank.'

19 September

In an effort to clamp down on juvenile offenders, Home Secretary Jack Straw unveiled plans to give courts the power to impose fines or even prison sentences on parents who fail to control their children.

'…and another thing. I got home at midnight last night - NO SUPPER! Then I've had to play truant all morning without breakfast…' *22 September*

Faced with a threatened revolt by backbenchers, Opposition leader William Hague sent out a postal ballot on his reform package to the entire Party membership, urging Conservatives nationwide to 'back me or sack me'.

'And so in answer to his call "back me or sack me", let us rally together, united in our support for Mr…Mr…you know, little thingy with the bald head and baseball cap…' *23 September*

In Saudi Arabia, British nurses Lucille McLauchlan and Deborah Parry were found guilty of murdering an Australian colleague and faced the death penalty or public flogging followed by long prison sentences.

'Dear Judge. Remember me cursing you for that 15-year sentence? Please accept my sincere apologies and the enclosed £20 note...' *25 September*

After introducing controversial new regulations, the Amateur Boxing Association officially sanctioned a fight of three 90-second rounds by two 13-year-old schoolgirls from Stoke-on-Trent.

'…You were just saying…"Little girls should learn to knit, not box come on, girly, take a swipe at me, get through my guard."' *2 October*

The Government announced plans to replace Britain's strict animal quarantine system with a 'pet passport' scheme certifying that a pet was resident in Europe and had been vaccinated against rabies.

'Good Lord, no. We're not made of money. My husband couldn't afford to come.' *3 October*

Marks & Spencer became the first major food chain to declare that it would only sell free-range eggs in its 285 British and 20 French stores.

'Personally, I preferred it when they sold battery eggs.' *7 October*

Speaking at a fringe meeting during the Conservative Party conference in Blackpool, former Chairman Norman Tebbit attacked multi-culturalism, saying that it could turn Britain into 'another Yugoslavia'.

'Oh, very well, I do solemnly swear I am in favour of a multi-cultural, live-and-let-live society. I do not know Lord Tebbit or any other Tebbits, my children do not play with Tebbits, I have never voted for a Tebbit...'

9 October

At another fringe meeting, former Defence Secretary Michael Portillo challenged Tory policy regarding the traditional family unit and appealed for a more liberal approach to sex in both politics and society in general.

'And so, fellow Conservatives, let us raise our glasses to Michael Portillo and a new era of sexual tolerance...' *10 October*

Piers Merchant, Tory MP for Beckenham, Kent, resigned after the *Sunday Mirror* revealed that he had renewed his relationship with an 18-year-old nightclub hostess during the Blackpool conference.

'I'm fed up with it, Piers. Most men nod off with a good book or by watching TV.' *14 October*

Home Secretary Jack Straw introduced a controversial new Crime and Disorder Bill which would give magistrates the power to lock up tearaways as young as 12 to prevent them reoffending before coming to court.

'Oi, Fingers - your turn to tell 'im a story. I did it last night.' *16 October*

England soccer captain Glenn Hoddle separated from his wife and received counselling from faith-healer Eileen Drewery, who had allegedly cured him of a hamstring injury in 1975.

'Hang on, Glenn. The spirits are with us. A message is coming through the ether...'
17 October

During the Queen's tour of India to mark the 50th anniversary of Independence, a speech she had prepared to give at a banquet in Chennai, formerly Madras, was cancelled.

'Won't keep you long. She's determined not to waste that speech which was cancelled in Madras.'

20 October

The *Sun* revealed that the Duchess of York had written letters to the Royal Family asking them to forgive her past misdemeanours. Meanwhile, the Royal Yacht *Britannia* made a farewell tour of the UK before being decommissioned.

'I wonder if we can arrange something similar for the Duchess of York?' *21 October*

A Church court in Caernafon heard how a 49-year-old married priest with three children had invited a young mother to join a three-in-a-bed romp with his 56-year-old mistress.

'For what I am about to receive, may the Lord make me truly thankful…' *23 October*

The Prime Minister was booed on a visit to the City of London after shares crashed over uncertainty about European monetary union. Meanwhile, 147 Tory MPs returned from a successful 'bonding' weekend' at a hotel in Eastbourne.

'They've done their bonding. Now they're back for a three-day gloating weekend.' *24 October*

The German motor manufacturer BMW, which bought Rover in 1994, was tipped as being the most likely purchaser of Rolls-Royce. In the event, Vickers sold the company to Volkswagen.

'I hope you're not thinking of turning up at the club in that load of foreign rubbish, Farquharson!' *28 October*

Public Service Minister Peter Kilfoyle announced that the Grade One-listed Admiralty Arch building near Buckingham Palace was to be turned into a cold-weather shelter for up to 60 young homeless people.

'I say, you up there. Will you turn that music down? One is trying to get some sleep.'
30 October

William Hague's tough stance against a single currency split the newly united Tory party and led to the resignation of Shadow Agriculture Minister David Curry and Northern Ireland spokesman Ian Taylor.

'Looks like the Tories have just had another bonding session.' *31 October*

Former Chancellor of the Exchequer Kenneth Clark joined the fray over Conservative policy on Europe and erstwhile Deputy Prime Minister Michael Heseltine made an outspoken attack on William Hague in an interview on breakfast television.

'What a shame, Michael. You were doing so well trying to kick the habit. You haven't stabbed a leader in the back since Margaret Thatcher.' *3 November*

The Channel ports in France were blocked by a French truck-drivers' strike. Back in the UK, tough visa controls were planned when nearly 600 Czech and Slovakian gypsies arrived at Dover in a single week.

'You 'eard me. Nip out, climb the ladder, open the hatch, toss your thermos and crisps in, then tell the 75 Slovak gypsies in there you've got some bad news.' *4 November*

A voluntary agreement was made between the Government and industry to cease the testing of cosmetics on animals in Britain.

'The wife got him from one of them laboratories where they used to test cosmetics...'

7 November

Tension grew in the Gulf as the USA threatened military action against Iraq for impeding UN arms inspectors. Meanwhile, legal history was made when the verdict in the trial of nanny Louise Woodward was announced on the Internet.

'Nothing so far on Louise Woodward, Illustrious One. But there's a strange message from Clinton for you.'
10 November

There was an outcry over news that motor-racing supremo Bernie Ecclestone, who had put pressure on the Government to exempt Formula 1 from the ban on tobacco sponsorship, had donated over £5,000 to the Labour Party.

'Exciting news, ladies and gentlemen. Apparently, if we donate over £5,000 to the Labour Party, we're in with a chance of being sponsored by one of the tobacco giants.' *11 November*

The Association of Teachers and Lecturers advised its 160,000 members to "bash and dash" as a last resort if threatened by aggressive pupils or parents, aiming blows at the knee, solar plexus, elbow or little finger.

'We had the knee, elbow and little finger yesterday. I think today must be solar plexus.'

13 November

The Court of Appeal heard how a 29-year-old Iranian man, a self-confessed 'inveterate lecher', wished to claim asylum in Britain to avoid being stoned to death or flogged for adultery in his home country.

'He comes in most nights to get stoned for adultery.' *14 November*

Prime Minister Tony Blair apologized on BBC TV's 'On the Record' programme for the Government's mistakes in its handling of the decision to exempt Formula 2 motor-racing from the ban on tobacco sponsorship of sport.

'Hey, look. A new Government warning - the Prime Minister is really, really sorry you're going to have to die.'

17 November

New league tables showed that grant-maintained schools, which had opted out of local council control, took six out of the top 10 places for GCSE results. Meanwhile, the row about tobacco sponsorship of sport continued.

'I sometimes wonder where our Labour council gets the money for its grants.' *18 November*

As part of the Golden Wedding anniversary celebrations for the Queen and Prince Philip a 'People's Banquet' was held for 350 guests during which commoners sat with royalty.

'Great time, Liz and Phil. For next year's People's Banquet it's everyone round to our place.' *21 November*

Fenn Chapman, a 16-year-old pupil at Rugby public school, ran away to Barbados, where he had spent a family holiday at the luxurious Sandey Lane Hotel the previous year.

'Ah, young Chapman. We've decided you're right. We hate school too and have decided to join you - shall we start with maths?' *25 November*

There was a new twist in the divorce battle between Earl Spencer and his wife when his former mistress, Chantal Collopy, sided with Lady Spencer in her legal suit to prove that he was a serial adulterer.

'Oi! Get yer hands off! Who d'you think you are - Lord Spencer?' *27 November*

In his will Cheshire mattress millionaire Donald Moss bequeathed £50,000 to his nextdoor neighbour to care for his 52-year-old tortoise, Big Tibby.

'It's only for the winter. Bless him, he's hibernating.' *28 November*

Hard-line Unionists were furious when they learnt that Sinn Fein representatives Gerry Adams and Martin McGuinness were to be invited to Downing Street for talks in an attempt to keep the Ulster peace process moving.

'The Unionists will be protestin' outside the gates, Gerry. Besides, we think this is a fitting way for you both to arrive at No. 10.' *1 December*

Angry farmers and butchers accused Agriculture Minister Jack Cunningham of overreaction when the Government imposed a ban on the sale of beef on the bone as an added precaution against BSE.

'Oh, ma wishbone's connected to ma shoulderbone, ma shoulderbone's connected to ma chestbone ...'

4 December

While a new Government initiative to reduce truancy amongst schoolchildren was welcomed, Labour backbenchers rebelled over a proposed cut in benefits to single parents.

'I'm not sure whether they're after me for being a single parent or you for playing truant.' *9 December*

The Government threatened to boycott all BBC news and current affairs programmes after Social Security Secretary Harriet Harman was repeatedly interrupted by interviewer John Humphrys on Radio 4's *Today*.

'Mr Humphrys. We've been sent by the Labour Party. Congratulations, you're just about to qualify for disabled benefits...' *16 December*

Supported by their customers, some family butchers decided to openly flout the Government's beef-on-the-bone ban, risking a £2,000 fine or up to two years in prison.

'The big parcel's from Uncle Glyn, the butcher. But he says no feeling it or you might guess...' *18 December*

Tory leader William Hague and his wife Ffion Jenkins spent their honeymoon at the Lake Palace in Rajasthan. Meanwhile a storm was brewing in Westminster over proposed cuts to welfare benefits for the disabled.

'Oh no. Here he comes again! Yesterday I got one whole rupee and an hour's lecture on how the Labour leader would have cut that in half...' *22 December*

The Government stirred up further discontent over the disability payments issue when it alleged that some of those claiming Incapacity Benefit were in fact capable of work.

'Wake up, Mr Bainbridge. Time for your window-cleaning round...' *23 December*

An inquiry into the murder of Loyalist terrorist Billy 'King Rat' Wright inside the Maze Prison, Belfast, revealed that some aspects of security had been relaxed in order to gain the prisoners' support for the peace process.

'Two Smith & Wesson pizzas for Cell Block 22a with 16mm dumdum and mozzarella topping - that seems okay. In you go…' *29 December*

In Hong Kong 1.3 million chickens were slaughtered to prevent the spread of the killer 'bird flu' virus. Meanwhile scores of illegal Kurdish refugees intercepted in Italy said that they had been heading for Britain.

'These aren't Kurdish refugees, Captain. I think they're from Hong Kong.' *30 December*

Pop star Elton John, who had sung at Princess Diana's funeral, received a knighthood in the New Year Honour's list.

'Sir Elton. Can you pop back for a moment please?' *1 January*

A priest who had agreed to bless an eight-stone rottweiler in a special service at All Saints' Church, Lincoln, backed out when it became clear that its owner really wanted the dog to be baptised.

'And so, after much soul-searching and a little persuasion, I baptise this dog...' *2 January*

Britain suffered its worst storms since the 1987 hurricane. Ferocious winds blowing at speeds of up to 115 mph battered the whole country, causing widespread destruction, floods and power cuts.

'I've been meaning to ask you. When do you think we should take the decorations down?' *5 January*

Professor Michael Barber, head of the Government's School Effectiveness Unit, announced plans to invite private businesses to take over the running of hundreds of inner-city schools.

'Isn't that exciting, children? Today we're going to build a new dual carriageway near Maidstone. So get yourself a little pick or shovel...' *8 January*

In a bid to prevent their political representatives from walking out of the all-party peace talks, Northern Ireland Secretary Mo Mowlam visited Loyalist terrorists in Belfast's Maze Prison.

'Listen. I've got a snooker tournament, a massage and manicure, the wife's visit, then the girlfriend's visit - tell Mo Mowlam I can only spare her five minutes...' *9 January*

Social Security Secretary Harriet Harman introduced an 'affluence test' for pregnant women - who receive 90 per cent of their salary in state benefits for the first six weeks of maternity leave - in order to cut payments to high earners.

'Scuse me, yhour lordship. About these maternity benefit cuts. Does 'Arriet 'Arman means test you or me?'
13 January

The North Yorkshire Training and Enterprise Council offered free one-hour lessons on the quickest way to put on a duvet cover.

'Isn't that amazing, darling? Someone's filled and done up the duvet in under three minutes...' *15 January*

Two Ginger Tamworth pigs, later christened Butch and Sundance, escaped from an abattoir in Malmesbury, Wiltshire. They were eventually captured and, sponsored by the *Daily Mail*, transferred to an animal sanctuary.

'That's right, Constable. He took my wallet, my passport, my car… and you're not going to believe the next bit…' *16 January*

New claims of sexual misdemeanours at the White House came to light during the long-running investigation into US President Clinton's alleged sexual harrassment of a colleague while Governor of Arkansas.

'Mr President. Meet ex-nurse Wilma McLuskey. Arkansas Maternity Hospital 1946. Claims to have seen you without your nappy many times - will settle for a million bucks.' *20 January*

The Queen Mother, aged 97, was taken to King Edward VII Hospital, London, after she fell and fractured her left hip as she watched horses at the Royal Stud at Sandringham in Norfolk.

'Dammit, nurse. You and your rules! You could have allowed her just one gin and tonic.'

27 January

Jockeys Jamie Osborne, Dean Gallagher and Leighton Aspell were arrested after dope tests on two horses, Avanti Express and Lively Knight, proved positive.

'Break it to me gently. What and how much of it was in that last syringe?' *29 January*

Fears about the effects of global warming grew as scientists reported that a slab of ice the size of Norfolk had broken off the 1,700-square-mile Larsen B ice-shelf in Antarctica.

'Listen to this, Lizzie. A piece of ice bigger than Norfolk has broken away from Antarctica.'
30 January

Tony Blair flew to Washington for a conference with the US President over Iraq's refusal to allow UN weapons inspectors access to its military sites. Meanwhile further details of Bill Clinton's sex life were revealed.

'Cherie's busy right now. She's being fitted with a new outfit for when we meet Clinton on Wednesday.'

2 February

As tension in the Gulf escalated, Foreign Secretary Robin Cook visited Saudi Arabia for talks. Back home scandal erupted when news broke of his adulterous relationship with his secretary, Gaynor Regan.

'Welcome to Saudi Arabia, Mr Cook. We do hope you won't be flying home unexpectedly for any reason during our talks.' *5 February*

The Government released information on the deadly biological and chemical weapons - including anthrax and nerve-gas - which it believed Saddam Hussein was hiding from UN weapons inspectors.

'Saddam, darling. Have you been hiding stuff from the weapons inspectors in our bathroom cabinet again?'
6 February

A spokesman for Harrod's, owned by Mohammed Al-Fayed, denied that his son Dodi had had a secret love-child with a Suffolk woman before beginning his relationship with Princess Diana.

'Dodi! Come back, yer little bleeder. I want yer to meet yer grandad.' *10 February*

At an industrial tribunal in Bristol 34-year-old Paul Burgess lost his claim for unfair dismissal when he was sacked as the Queen's hairdresser because she wanted a change of style.

'Hello, dear. How was the new man?' *12 February*

There was massive mobilization in the Gulf as the Allies threatened a full-scale blitz on Iraq's military bases. Meanwhile, Education Secretary David Blunkett announced a major new drive to reduce class sizes in schools.

'Isn't it exciting, children? The Prime Minister wants to cut down on class sizes - so he's sending half of you to Iraq.' *13 February*

Nearly 1,000 people were evacuated when a massive 1,000 lb unexploded German bomb dropped during the Second World War was discovered on the outskirts of Chippenham, Wiltshire.

'Winifred, dearest. Have you forgiven me for forgetting Valentine's Day yet?' *16 February*

Sculptor Antony Gormley's *The Angel of the North*, the biggest statue in Britain, was unveiled beside the A1 at Gateshead, Tyne and Wear. The 200-ton, 65-foot-high steel giant cost £800,000 and has a wingspan of 175 feet.

'No thanks, sir, we've eaten - can we have a word?' *17 February*

In an eleventh-hour move to try and defuse the excalating crisis in the Gulf, UN Secretary-General Kofi Annan flew to Baghdad to talk to Saddam Hussein personally about allowing access to his hidden weapons' stockpiles.

'You lazy slut! Look at the place! - What's the UN Secretary-General going to think?'
19 February

The Department of Health set up an emergency telephone helpline when it was revealed that up to 5,000 pensioners had been fitted with faulty hip joints manufactured by an American company based in Leicestershire.

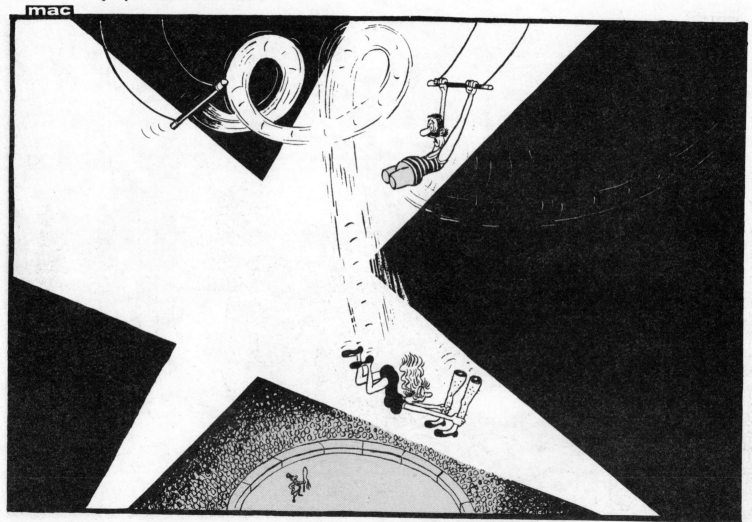

'Bad news, darling. I've just heard I've been fitted with faulty hip joints.' *20 February*

The UN's Kofi Annan succeeded in defusing the Gulf crisis. Meanwhile, in London, Minister Without Portfolio Peter Mandelson announced that the centrepiece of the Millennium Dome at Greenwich would be a giant human statue.

'Oh, God. The West are really putting on the pressure now. Bombing threats I can ignore, but then being stuffed and put in Peter Mandelson's Dome…!' *23 February*

Proposed new legislation against hunting with hounds triggered a widespread revolt against Government policy on rural issues in general. An estimated 250,000 protesters joined the Countryside March on London.

'This is the life. Before they get back from London, what d'you fancy for breakfast - the contents of their fridge or a few more chickens from the yard?' *2 March*

A man attending an investiture at Buckingham Palace needed nine stitches after being struck by ceiling plaster. It was also revealed for the first time that Camilla Parker Bowles had regularly stayed overnight at nearby St James's Palace.

'Nip upstairs and tell Charles and Camilla to stop whatever they're doing immediately.'

5 March

Industry watchdog Oftel ordered mobile phone companies to cut their charges when an
official investigation discovered that the cost of calls made by Britain's 7.3 million
customers were among the highest in the world.

'It's me, darling. Have you read the wonderful news?' *6 March*

Prince Philip was reported to be against further moves to modernize the Royal Family. Meanwhile there were rumours that Culture Secretary Chris Smith privately favoured restoring the Elgin Marbles to the Parthenon.

'Cheer up, Phil, old cock. It's not all bad news. You Greeks might be getting your marbles back.' *9 March*

A Government report issued on National No-Smoking Day officially confirmed that passive smoking can cause cancer and heart disease. Research also revealed that 8 million Britons were illiterate and innumerate.

' 'Ard to believe innit, Dad? There are eight million people in this country who're illiterate.'
12 March

As the 'Zippergate' presidential sex-scandal investigations continued, Bill Clinton bowed to public opinion and reluctantly allowed his Labrador puppy, Buddy, to be neutered.

'Oh, hi, big boy. Someone tells me you're paying a visit to the vet's tomorrow...'

13 March

Chancellor Gordon Brown's Budget increased the price of petrol by a further 6 per cent in a move criticised by the Automobile Association as 'anti-motorist'.

'Gad! How I miss my Rolls. I put half a gallon into this thing and it conked out.' *19 March*

Heart-throb *Titanic* film star Leonardo DiCaprio was in London for the opening of his new blockbuster, *The Man in the Iron Mask*, at the Odeon Cinema, Leicester Square.

'Honest, Tracey. There I was outside the Odeon Leicester Square when a voice says, "Ello, darlin', I'm Leonardo DiCaprio." Fantastic, eh? Mind you, he's put on a bit of weight.' *20 March*

In a dramatic gesture to protect his economic reforms from a possible backlash by
Communist hardliners, 67-year-old vodka-drinking Russian President, Boris Yeltsin,
dismissed his Prime Minister and his entire Cabinet.

'...Nobody against? Thank you, comrades, another motion carried. I declare this meeting over. Everyone
down to the bar...' *24 March*

When Medway Secure Training Centre for juvenile offenders opened near Cookham Wood, Kent, many protested at the high running costs and the lavish facilities which made it more like a hotel than a prison for young tearaways.

'We've given him everything. Toys, videos, constant love and affection - now he wants a few weeks' break at the Medway Secure Training Centre.' *16 April*

Prince Charles invited the Spice Girls to Highgrove House in Gloucestershire to have tea with their biggest royal fan. Prince Harry.

'You're a sport Camilla. After yesterday's tea with the Spice Girls, I didn't want things to go flat.' *17 April*

After the exposure of his multi-million pound offshore trust fund, Paymaster-General Geoffrey Robinson hit the headlines again when it was revealed that he had had an affair with an Italian actress.

'Come quickly. Mr Robinson's opera-singer wife is going to teach him how to shatter a wine glass with a high C.' *20 April*

An exhibition at the Science Museum highlighting the dangers of poor diet and insufficient exercise by modern youngsters included a tower of lard representing the amount of fat consumed by a single child in 10 years.

'Oi! That was an exhibit. The cafe is just down the corridor.' *21 April*

Public anger ran high when news leaked out that the Prime Minister had made a secret deal with President Clinton to reprocess deadly Soviet nuclear waste at Dounreay, Scotland, without consulting Parliament.

'I had a wee parcel from Russia for ye too, but it must've fallen off my bike.' *23 April*

The organisers of the 1998 Football World Cup were criticised over insufficient ticket allocation for non-French fans. And in a much-publicised move, England manager Glenn Hoddle invited faith-healer Eileen Drewery to help his team win.

'Oui, oui madame, your message is coming through... I am to put 10,000 tickets in an envelope and send them to M'sieur Hoddle's medium and faith healer, c/o Wembley Stadium...' *24 April*

Abel Anton from Spain won the 1998 Flora London Marathon in 2 hours 7 minutes and 57 seconds.

'Here he comes, last again - heads you tell him the car's been nicked and the dog's eaten his World Cup ticket...' *27 April*

Dr Lynne Jones, Labour MP for Birmingham Selly Oak, began a heated debate when she suggested that all women should experience sex before getting married.

'Sorry I'm late. I suddenly thought: that Labour MP is right. A girl shouldn't be a virgin when she gets married.'

28 April

A private clinic in Harley Street, London, became the first surgery in Britain to prescribe the new American anti-impotence drug Viagra. Meanwhile, the Embassy World Snooker Championships reached the quarter-final stage.

'I'm worried, doctor. He's acting very strangely... swallowed a lot of pills and hasn't switched on the snooker...' *30 April*

The Ulster peace talks were held up when the IRA refused to discuss the decommissioning of arms - a central issue for Loyalist support of the Good Friday Agreement. Meanwhile Viagra continued to hit the headlines.

'It's every man's fear - becoming impotent.' *1 May*

William Hague hoped for a revival of Tory fortunes in the local elections. Londoners were also asked to vote on whether they were in favour of a directly elected mayor - one contender being former GLC Chairman Ken Livingstone.

'Please, folks. I'm relying on your votes - after all, most of you were Tory MPs only a year ago.' *7 May*

There was a storm of controversy when Foreign Secretary Robin Cook denied
all knowledge of a British company's involvement in supplying arms to
mercenaries restoring President Kabbah to power in Sierra Leone.

'Here it is in a letter I wrote to you two months ago - "My darling Robin. You were wonderful tonight, I love you
snookum wookums… P.S. Somebody rang about sending arms to Sierra Leone and I said okay…" ' *11 May*

Republicans rejoiced when four major IRA terrorists were freed on parole by the Irish Government after being transferred from Belfast to Dublin as part of the Ulster peace process.

'Not much hope of an early release for me - I'm in for shoplifting.' *12 May*

War veterans, including Prince Philip - President of the Burma Star Association - were unhappy about the Queen's decision to confer the Order of the Garter on Japanese Emperor Akihito during his official visit to the UK.

'Thanks for the advice Philip. But I'll just be giving the emperor the usual light tap on the shoulder.' *14 May*

Actor and singer Frank Sinatra died aged 82 in Los Angeles, California. He was the last of the infamous hellraising 'Rat Pack' of showbusiness friends that also included Dean Martin, Sammy Davis Junior and Peter Lawford.

'You just missed it. Man, what a party - the Rat Pack are together again.' *18 May*

In a remarkable break with decorum the Queen, a 72-year-old grandmother, sprinted across the paddock to watch Prince Philip performing in the Asprey's Carriage Driving Grand Prix at the Royal Windsor Horse Show.

'Let's hope this new running thing is only going to be a passing phase.' *19 May*

Having escaped a public flogging for the murder of a colleague in Saudi Arabia, British nurses Lucille McLauchlan and Deborah Parry flew home amid rumours that they had sold their stories to the media for vast sums.

A Public Flogging *21 May*

News of the Queen's planned visit to Dublin - the first by a British monarch for 85 years
- coincided with a high-profile campaign by major British politicians to secure a 'Yes'
vote in the referendum on the Good Friday Agreement.

'Bejasus! First it's Tony Blair blatherin' on about a "Yes" vote, then John Major, then Hague. Who is it now?'

22 May

More than 70 per cent of voters backed the peace deal for Ulster outlined in the Good Friday Agreement. However, some Unionist leaders, such as the Reverend Ian Paisley, were still unhappy with the result.

'It's your wife, Mr Paisley, sir. Are you coming home soon? This is your sixth recount.' *25 May*

In an interview on BBC Radio 4's 'Today' programme, Health Secretary Frank Dobson denied Tory claims that 62 hospitals had been earmarked for closure.

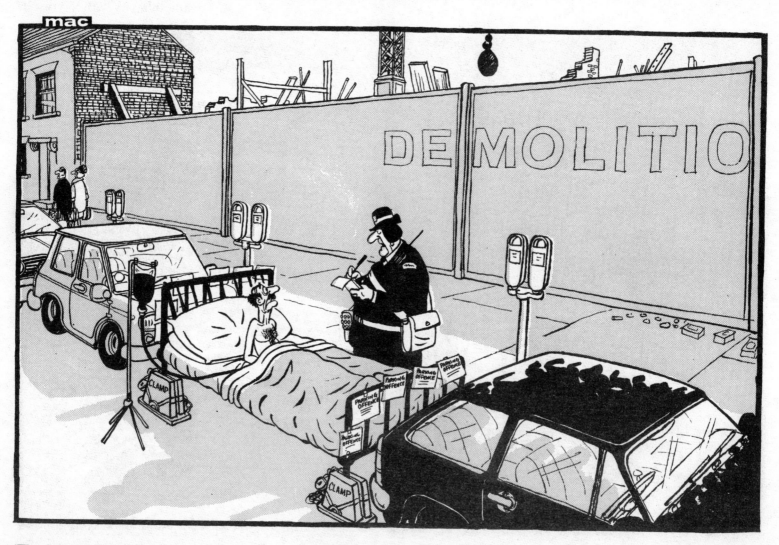

'The hospital? Oh dear. Frank Dobson must've had it pulled down and this road built while you were under the anaesthetic, luv.' *28 May*

Only two weeks after India exploded its first atomic bombs, Pakistan followed suit,
detonating five nuclear devices in Chagal near the Afghan border.

'He wouldn't have done that before he became a nuclear power!' *29 May*

25-year-old Geri Halliwell split from the Spice Girls pop group while on a concert tour in Norway. Meanwhile, it was rumoured that Northern Ireland Secretary Mo Mowlam had invited members of Sinn Fein to a Royal Garden Party.

'Honestly, Martin, these Brits! How Mo Mowlam could throw a garden party at a time like this beats me...'

1 June

The Spice Girls decided to continue their concert tour without their fifth member. Back home, Glenn Hoddle dropped soccer star Paul 'Gazza' Gascoigne from the England World Cup squad as he was deemed unfit.

'Sorry, duckies. It was a good idea but he's just not fit enough.' *2 June*

Denise van Outen, presenter of Channel 4 TV's 'The Big Breakfast', admitted stealing a glass ashtray and other 'mementoes' of the occasion when she attended a royal reception for young achievers at Buckingham Palace.

'Apart from that ashtray, have you noticed anything else missing since Monday's young achievers reception?'

4 June

The Law Lords moved to remedy the situation when it was revealed that four leading barristers had charged huge fees for legal aid work paid for by the state.

'Bad news, Lucinda darling. We may have to cut back. They're thinking of restricting my legal aid fees.'

5 June

The 16th Football World Cup Finals kicked off in Paris with a match between Scotland and Brazil (Brazil won 2-1).

'Hello. It's me, Ethel. Open your mouth - your dinner's on the way...' *11 June*

Liberal Democrat MP Dr Jenny Tonge tabled a Commons motion to make the 'morning after' contraceptive pill available without prescription.

'You don't by any chance sell a "sixteen years after" pill, do you?' *12 June*

England soccer hooligans ran riot in Marseilles on the eve of the nation's first World Cup match against Tunisia. Back home, many businesses were affected by absenteeism as sports fans watched the match on TV.

'Good Lord! What an extraordinary coincidence. My entire workforce are attending their grandmothers' funerals today too.' *15 June*

England beat Tunisia 2-1 in Marseilles. Meanwhile, a survey of American users of the anti-impotency drug Viagra revealed that some perfectly healthy couples were using it as a fast-acting aphrodisiac.

'It's six days now. Have those Viagra pills started working yet?' *16 June*

Maverick Tory MP Alan Clark was widely condemned for appearing to justify the behaviour of England's football hooligans in France, arguing on Radio 4's 'Today' programme that they had been the victims of unprovoked attacks.

'Gentlemen. Be upstanding for the loyal toast - to Alan Clark.' *18 June*

When President of the Board of Trade, Margaret Beckett, announced that the new national minimum wage for adults would be set at £3.80 per hour, angry union leaders declared that it was 'an endorsement of workplace poverty'.

'It's no use moaning to me, Doris. You should let the Prime Minister know how you feel about the minimum wage.' *19 June*

To the dismay of historians, it was reported that the Queen Mother had allowed Princess Margaret to burn a large number of her personal letters and private papers stored at Clarence House.

'Bad news about your private papers, ma'am. Princess Margaret has smoked the lot.' *22 June*

Romania beat England 2-1 in Toulouse. Back home, despite dissent from Church leaders and others, the House of Commons voted to lower the age of consent for homosexuals from 18 to 16.

'Who cares who won? Have the Commons lowered the age of consent for gays?' *23 June*

Rupert Murdoch's pro-Labour tabloid the *Sun* printed a photo of Tony Blair with the caption 'Is this the most dangerous man in Britain?' and attacked the Government for changing its policy on a single European currency.

'Sorry, luv. I think Murdoch's swinging back to the Tories.' *25 June*

Football continued to dominate the headlines. In an unprecedented move to stop crowd violence, French authorities imposed a 24-hour ban on the sale of alcohol in Calais and Lens ahead of England's match against Colombia.

'Removez le chapeau, mate. They want to 'ave a look at yer 'at.' *26 June*

As well as success on the football pitch England scored well at Wimbledon, with Tim Henman getting through to the quarter-finals. At the Glastonbury pop festival in Somerset constant rain turned the site into a quagmire.

'England beat Colombia and Henman's through to the next round - how was it at Glastonbury?' *29 June*

Nude radio made its debut when an edition of BBC Radio 4's 'Gardeners' Question Time' was recorded before a naked audience.

'No, Mr Winthrop. I'm not listening to "Gardeners' Question Time" right now - why?' *30 June*

Old memories of the Falklands War were revived for some when England faced
Argentina in the World Cup. England lost on a penalty shoot-out having been reduced to
10 men after David Beckham was sent off for kicking a player.

**'In the early hours of this morning, a young man named David Beckham was savagely attacked with this blunt
instrument… a woman is helping with inquiries.'** *2 July*

46-year-old Robert Fraser, Head of Religious Education at a school in Bournemouth, Dorset, was suspended from duty when it was discovered that he earned £1000 a week working as a male stripper in his spare time.

'Your old R. E. teacher may be earning £1000 a week doing that, headmaster. But your topic tonight was: "The Aztecs. Did they have marmalade?" - fee twenty pounds.' *3 July*

Thousands of Protestant Orangemen who defied a ban and attempted to march through Catholic areas of Drumcree to celebrate the 309th anniversary of the Battle of the Boyne were stopped by a massive police and army presence.

'Earth probe calling, Earthprobe calling. We are returning to base. No sign of intelligent life here.' *6 July*

'Anyone know where we can get some Viagra?' *9 July*

France beat Croatia in Paris to appear in their first ever Football World Cup Final and
then stunned audiences around the globe by going on to beat favourites Brazil 3-0.

**'So sorry, M'sieur. We appear to 'ave run out of the 1972 Chateauneuf du Pape - een fact we 'ave run out of
everysing.'** *10 July*

Chancellor Gordon Brown announced that an extra £20 billion would be spent on the NHS over the next three years. However, at the same time, pay for health workers would be kept on a tight rein.

'Ah, well. Can't drown our sorrows all day. One more and it's time to go to work… hello, where's the patient?'

16 July

Seven life-insurance salesmen needed hospital treatment after attempting to walk across hot coals during a 'motivation course' at a hotel near Cheltenham, Gloucestershire.

'Dammit, Donald. Motivation courses may be the in thing, but we only want the lad to deliver newspapers.'
17 July

When it was reported that the 'Volvo run' accounted for a fifth of all rush-hour traffic, Deputy Prime Minister John Prescott launched a crackdown on parents who ferry their children to and from school by car.

'I've just broken the news to him that, after today, Mr Prescott's probably going to make him walk to school.'

20 July

Though passed by the House of Commons, the House of Lords rejected the proposal to lower the age of consent for homosexuals from 18 to 16.

'I've no idea, son - why do you want to know how the House of Lords vote went...?' *23 July*

It was announced that the Russians were planning to launch a satellite equipped with a 25-metre reflector dish to beam light ten times stronger than a full moon into the darkest parts of Siberia.

'There goes that damned Russian space-mirror again, reflecting the sun's rays!' *24 July*

In Tony Blair's first Cabinet reshuffle, Agriculture Minister Jack Cunningham was promoted to the job of Minister for the Cabinet Office, to act as 'enforcer' amongst potential front-bench rebels.

'The Prime Minister's new appointment is here bearing news of the reshuffle - I think it's either Arnold Schwarzenegger or Jack Cunningham...' *27 July*

In a bid to control classroom thugs, the Government issued new guidelines to teachers which allowed them to use 'reasonable force' against violent or unruly pupils.

'CAN'T YOU WAIT TILL THE SCHOOL HOLIDAYS ARE OVER?' *28 July*

A research institute in Cambridge announced that it planned to start clinical trials on the use of pigs' livers as a type of life-support system for humans.

'Apart from a few little side-effects, Bernard's pig-organ transplant is working well.' *31 July*

The Essential Gluten Baking Guide

PART 1 Learn how to use Amaranth, Almond, Quinoa, Garbanzo, Millet and Coconut Flour in 50+ recipes

TriumphDining

Brittany Angell
Iris Higgins

The Essential Gluten-Free Baking Guide
by Brittany Angell & Iris Higgins

Copyright ©2012 by Triumph Dining
http://www.triumphdining.com

ISBN 978-0977611140

Book cover design by Jeff Weeks
Photos by Matt Calabrese, Calabrese Studios
Interior design and layout by Val Sherer, Personalized Publishing Services

Triumph Dining
144 Diablo Ranch Court, Danville, CA 94506 USA

Table of Contents

Acknowledgments

This book would not have been possible without a number of people and companies. We give our heartfelt thanks to:

JK Gourmet, Honeyville Grains, Dakota Prairie, Nuts.com, Big Tree Farms, Simply Organic, Navitas Naturals, Shiloh Farms and Garden of Life

Photography: Matt Calabrese

Videography: Bruce Begy

Researchers: Ashley Ayres, Season Fagan

Recipe Formatting: Alexis Mettler

Baking Assistant: Maia A'Brams Horvath

Recipe Testers: Christine Holzmann, Jessica L. Angell, Laurel VanBlarcum, Gina Pagano, Sherman Sherman, Linda Stiles, Betsy Higgins, Alta Mantsch, Kim Boggs, Deanna Schneider, Julia Simpson, Sarah Stivers, Angela Kuhn, Suzanne Hill, Lindsay Keach, Georgianna Reilly, Jessica Rodgers, Ginger Garza, Noelle Rose, Ricki Heller, Julia Berger, Laura King, Erica Nafziger, Amanda Hockham, Ande Baker, Deborah Baca-Dietz, Emily Smith, Tessa Thralls, Abby Pattison, Tre Gallery, Rose Myers, Rebecca Haacke, Jen Repard, Abbie Brown, Christine Nygren, Maggie Savage, Heather Graffam, Debi Smith, Teresa Wright, Alexa Croft, Jennifer Brunett, Katrina Morales, Alea Milham, Stephanie Laidlaw, Brooke Lippy, Zoe Hastings, Olivia Davis, Diane Eblin, Kalinda Piper, Heather Riley, Lisa Chalfant, Elizabeth Howes, Anney Ryan, Adriane Angarano, Amy Fratto, Jillian Punska, Heidi Kelly, Beverly Lane, Terri Tremblett, Krista Brouwer, Kristin Batson, Amy Harms Munson, Tina Pruett, Jey Rodgers, Dana Hantel, Jenni Schneider, Sherry Varano, Dr. Jennifer Feather, Kris Weimer, Kaitlyn Renfrow, Selene Nemethy-Fekete, Crystal Braylor

This book was a labor of love that was made with so many helping hands. Brittany, you are an amazing and devoted baker. Thank you, Rich, for keeping Brittany sane, and for your late night edits and countless taste tests. Thank you Dave Morris and Triumph Dining for giving us the creative freedom to make this book.

My family, I love you and credit you all for making me the person I am. Ladies of the Kenmore Estate, past and present, thank you for giving up your kitchen, for countless taste testings, and for your support. Lily, Hayley, my Tufts crew, and Micaela and Sarah, thank you for supporting my dreams and cheering me on. Steve, The Daily Dietribe would not exist without you. The Krivicich Family, your love and support has meant more than you will ever know. Emareya and Steven, you bring me peace. Bastyr community, my professors, Doris, the wonderful staff: thank you for supporting this endeavor! All my teachers, from pre-school on, thank you for getting me to this point and teaching me so much!

To Calder, for giving me the freedom to follow my dreams, and for following yours.

Iris Higgins

The past few years of my life have been a whirlwind of gifts of kindness. The following people helped to propel the dream that was this book into reality:

Iris Higgins, you are a true friend and confidant, a woman with an incredible work ethic and dedication. You inspired me, challenged me to work harder, and questioned me when others might be too afraid to do so. Thank you for your continual support, encouragement and honesty. I could not have asked for a better partner in crime!

Jason Berardi, you placed into my life a platform that allowed me to dance. John Maggio led me to Triumph Dining via Pam Sherman.

Dave Morris and Triumph Dining, thank you for taking a chance on me.

Don and Julie Riling, my parents, have provided me with their love and a confidence in spite of my stubborn nature. Brenton Riling, my brother, I appreciate all the help you have given me with Real Sustenance.

My husband, Rich Angell, has provided humor and willingness to taste every single item our oven produced. You have been my rock through my dramatic ups and downs over the many failures and successful baking quests. You encourage me and keep me humble.

Clyde and Chloe, my beloved Rat Terriers, you are a constant source of happiness and my daily companions in the kitchen!

Brittany Angell

Foreword

. . . .

Anything is possible with patience and perseverance. The first time I met Brittany and Iris I could see the fire in their eyes.

Like most of us, you came here out of necessity. You arrive open to learning a new way of eating, invigorated by the hope of restored energy and health. But with all of the possibilities come unknowns—unless you're armed with knowledge that only arises from experience.

The greatest mystery—whether you're newly diagnosed or have been living gluten-free for decades—is the vast selection of gluten-free flours. At first the abundance is exhilarating but it quickly becomes overwhelming when you realize that you're not sure what to do with any of them. You need a starting point.

That's where *The Essential Gluten-Free Baking Guides* come to your rescue. The authors have painstakingly tested 12 gluten-free flours, profiling taste, texture and best uses. They offer valuable baking tips, nutritional profiles and substitutions. Their guide will only lead you to baking greatness, and the thankful realization that they've done the heavy lifting for you. Now all you have to do is soak in the knowledge.

Silvana Nardone, Founding Editor-in-Chief of *Rachael Ray Magazine,* author of *Cooking for Isaiah: Gluten-Free & Dairy-Free Recipes for Easy, Delicious Meals* and SilvanasKitchen.com.

Introduction

My life changed on one cold morning in February 2010. I woke up with a pain in my side that would not subside. The call to my primary care doctor began a year-long process of going from specialist to specialist. I was prescribed various meds, my gallbladder was taken out and still my health continued to decline. Finally I took personal control of my health. The more I learned the more I wanted to learn. After several months I discovered I had severe food sensitivities and Hashimoto's Disease. I took the diagnosis in stride and took my research into the kitchen. My life's passion was found. Being in the kitchen experimenting with different ingredients and meals lit my soul on fire.

As I talked about my health with my friends, they encouraged me to share my knowledge. My website, www.RealSustenance.com, was born. It quickly took over my life. There were thousands of people struggling with many of the same issues and helping them helped me.

I'll never forget the first day I wandered into the gluten-free section of Wegmans, the local grocery store. There were so many bags of different types of gluten-free flour lining the shelves. Upon going gluten free, I revisited that section at Wegmans. I stared at the shelves. What should I buy? How did I use them? It didn't matter. My health was at stake. I filled the cart with those cute little one pound bags. Little did I realize they would also empty my bank account! I then walked to the bookstore down the street for some more education.

There wasn't a single book that had the information I needed on how to use the flours. I'm no trained chef and there were no elaborate instructions on the bags. All I wanted was to make delicious food to share with my husband.

As many of you have done, I began experimenting with different recipes. It took me nearly 6 months of constant baking to learn how to make anything of quality. Around this time I nailed a cake recipe that was exceptional. The response to this cake from others blew me away. It was then that I knew there must be a need for these types of recipes.

Iris Higgins came into my life soon after I started blogging. She was on a similar journey. We became fast friends, never anticipating what was to come. One day, during a random conversation on Facebook, the subject of coconut flour came up. We began conversing over the fact that this flour was confusing for both of us. From that seed grew the idea and ultimate fruition of these books.

We committed ourselves entirely to the creation of these books. We baked and baked. Recipes were developed slowly and tested multiple times. We tried them with different flours, sugars, dairy replacements, and with and without xanthan gum. We had one giant learning curve to work through. We wanted to save others time, frustration and money. We hope that our hard work provides you with the skills and abilities to give that same satisfaction to your loved ones.

We hope that the pages you're about to read inspire and excite you, and prepare you with the knowledge to step into the kitchen with confidence. We believe that anything can be made gluten- and allergen-free. When there's a will, there's always, always a way.

Brittany Angell

Chapter 1

How to Use This Book

· ·

We developed *The Essential Guides* to help you understand how each of the gluten-free flours work. Our goal was to help you get a handle on the flavor, texture and weight attributes that the flours give to baked goods. There are numerous gluten-free flours on the market, and usually a dozen can be found in your local grocery store. We selected a group that we felt were the most accessible and dedicated each chapter of these guides to a different flour. Our recipes have been formatted in the following way:

- Each recipe has been limited to the use of the featured flour, rice flour and the starches (tapioca, arrowroot or potato starch). The rice flour and starches play a background role in these recipes and allow the featured flour to show off its best qualities.

- We recommend preparing several recipes from each chapter to get a handle on the flour's taste and texture. Tasting the different flours in the recipes is important to the learning process. Plus, we have a hunch that you really might enjoy eating it all because it tastes so good!

- To keep things simple, our ingredients lists call for butter and milk. However, you can feel confident that we tested all of our recipes with dairy-free ingredients as well. When a recipe calls for butter, we have also tested it with Earth Balance Soy-Free Buttery Spread. When a recipe calls for milk, we have tested it with a variety of dairy-free milks, including almond, hemp and soy milk. For more information on replacing dairy, see our dairy section later in this chapter.

- Buy a scale and use the gram measurements to achieve best results. If you choose to use measuring cups, our measurements will either say *lightly filled cup* or *packed cup*. Lightly filled means you should scoop flour into your measuring cup and then level it off with a knife. Packed means you can scoop your measuring cup straight into the bag of flour. For starches and ingredients such as cornmeal, it doesn't matter if you scoop or pack, you'll get approximately the same results either way.

- If a recipe specifies that an ingredient should be room temperature or chilled, make sure to follow that direction. Having an ingredient at the wrong temperature can mean the difference between a beautifully risen loaf of bread or a dense loaf with a collapsed crust.

- To achieve our results, it is imperative that you use only the ingredients that we specify, at least the first time you make it; you can experiment after that. Avoid assumptions that the ingredients you have on hand will give you positive results. For example: superfine rice flour gives entirely different results than regular rice flour. When our recipes specify unrefined granulated sugar, we have tested them with

Sucanat, turbinado cane sugar, coconut palm sugar, and xylitol.

- Everyone likes to experiment. We suggest any changes to recipes be made one at a time. Any change can drastically affect a recipe and if your change creates a flop you can easily backtrack to find out where you went wrong.

- Many of our recipes use double acting baking powder; it gives the best overall results. If you can't find it in your local store then order some from Bobsredmill.com. If this is not an option, regular baking power will work but your baked good will lack some rise.

- A quick note on storing flours. White rice flour and starches can be stored at room temperature. Store all other flours in the fridge or freezer to prevent rancidity.

- Baking is a science. Changes to any recipe will affect the outcome. If you do choose to make changes be sure to take notes! Don't be afraid of experimentation! There are no failed recipes, only opportunities to learn.

When to Use All-Purpose Mixes in Our Recipes

We haven't tested every recipe here with all-purpose mixes and cannot guarantee successful results. That said, pancakes, waffles, muffins and quick breads typically work well using all-purpose flour mixes. You can make substitutions by adding up the total cups of flour and starch in the recipe and replacing them with an equal amount (in cups) of your favorite all-purpose mix. We do not recommend using an all-purpose flour mix for any of our recipes containing almond flour, coconut flour, sweet rice flour, potato flour or cassava.

Understanding Baking Soda and Baking Powder

Baking soda and powder are both made from baking soda. Baking soda is a chemical leavener that must come into contact with an acid (such as buttermilk, lemon juice or vinegar) to generate the reaction needed to produce carbon dioxide. The carbon dioxide creates the rise we so desire from our gluten-free baked goods. However, not all recipes contain these acids, which is why some recipes require baking powder. Baking powder is baking soda combined with an acid and cornstarch. The cornstarch keeps the two ingredients dry and non-reactive until they are introduced to moisture.

You'll notice that some recipes require both baking soda and powder because the use of both guarantees that the baked good will rise. Some recipes call for baking soda, baking powder and an acid. Why? The reaction from the baking soda and vinegar occurs quickly in the baking process. However, the baking soda eventually neutralizes the acids. Upon this neutralization, the baking powder kicks in to provide

the rest of the "lift". Think of those volcanoes you made as a child. The initial burst of foam from the vinegar and baking soda quickly fizzled out. To keep the experiment going you had to add more. The same concept occurs in the oven. If you are combining baking soda and an acid in a recipe, it's important to move the baked good into the oven as quickly as possible after mixing. Many of our recipes use double acting baking powder to better guarantee that this added boost occurs in the oven.

Understanding White and Brown Rice Flour

It would be convenient to use a single flour to achieve perfect recipes. Unfortunately gluten-free baking simply doesn't work that way. A few flours can be used on their own but most often another flour or starch will need to be added for proper results.

Brown rice flour and white rice flour work similarly, but white rice flour is lower in fiber and other nutrients. Brown rice flour will make your recipes taste just a bit heartier,

which is why we like to use white rice flour in recipes that we want to be especially fluffy or delicate.

Recommended Brands:
- **Nuts.com**
- **Bobsredmill.com**

If you must avoid rice flour for allergy reasons we suggest you replace it with sorghum flour or millet flour for the most comparable results.

Superfine Rice Flour

This phenomenal flour goes into its own category. There is a huge difference between regular rice and superfine rice flour. The difference is in the milling process in which the grain is ground into flour. Superfine is far superior in quality as it has been finely ground. This superfine flour has many benefits in baking. It absorbs more liquid, and gives baked goods great texture and a better rise. A number of our recipes were designed to use superfine rice flour. It is absolutely essential that it is used in these instances; neglecting to do so will result in poor results.

Both brown and white rice flour can be purchased superfine. We did extensive testing with a number of brands and discovered that several companies do an exceptional job milling their flours. We noticed they had superfine qualities without being called superfine. Dakota Prairie rice flours fall into this category. Their brown and white rice flour worked wonderfully in all of our superfine applications. Therefore, we placed their brand into the superfine category.

The rice flour found at your neighborhood Asian grocery store also falls into the unlabeled superfine category. These are a terrific and inexpensive alternative (approximately $1 per pound) to some of the other flours. We use this flour cup for cup in place of superfine with perfect results every time.

Recommended Brands:
- **Authentic Foods Superfine (brown or white)**
- **Dakota Prairie (brown or white) Note: not titled superfine**
- **Rice Flour from Asian grocery stores**

Many gluten-free baked goods using rice flour have the tendency to lose their soft texture when they become cold. This can be solved by re-heating the baked good prior to serving.

Understanding the Starches: Tapioca, Potato, Arrowroot, and Cornstarch

Starches help lighten recipes and bind ingredients together. For the most part, the starches can be exchanged gram for gram or cup for cup. They each impart a slightly different texture and flavor. We often like to use a mix of tapioca and potato starch.

Tapioca Starch: Tends to make recipes like cookies both crispy and chewy. Using too much tapioca starch in your recipes can result in a gummy texture.

Potato Starch: Makes recipes a little lighter and fluffier than tapioca starch. We use it with breads and pancakes for extra lift. We've also found that potato starch soaks up more liquid in recipes than the other starches. We like to use it for crispy baked goods such as crackers.

Arrowroot Starch: Very similar to and can be substituted for tapioca starch. Arrowroot is not included in any of our recipes in this book for one reason: cost. Tapioca is much less expensive and equally as effective.

Cornstarch: Won't be found in our recipes for one word: corn. Corn allergies are widespread. In many recipes, cornstarch can be exchanged in place of tapioca or arrowroot starch.

Most people develop a preference for a starch they like best. We encourage you to experiment to discover your own starch preference.

The Great Debate
Cups (Volume) vs. Grams

Is the investment in a good quality scale worth it?

When you measure a cup of flour three times, you'll likely come out with three different numbers. Sometimes those measurements only differ by a few grams. Other times, they're off by 20 or 30 grams. We've had recipes work perfectly for one tester and fail for another because they measured their flours differently. With grams, you can be sure you're following our recipes exactly. We encourage you to closely follow the weight measurements in our recipes or you may get varied results. Plus, if you measure by weight, you cut down on dishes to wash because you simply measure all of your ingredients straight into one bowl.

If weight is so important then why do we include volume measurements? It's because we both use volume in our own baking. We keep track of our weight measurements so that we can reproduce recipes exactly from one time to the next. But when we're substituting one flour for another, we have found volume measurements work better for us. We know this is different from what most people will tell you, so let us explain.

In our research, we kept reading that in substituting one flour for another, you had to do it by weight, not volume. Yet in our own baking, we subbed by volume and never had a problem. Feeling confused by this, Iris decided to do a little experiment. She took our

Sesame Buckwheat Breakfast Cookie recipe and played around with substitutions. She replaced the buckwheat with an equal volume of sorghum flour. Then she made the cookies again, replacing the buckwheat with an equal weight of sorghum flour. She did this with various individual flours, and also with Bob's Red Mill All-Purpose Mix. The results were the same every time. When she subbed in another flour by volume, the resulting cookie came out similarly to the original. When she subbed in another flour by weight, the batter was thinner and the cookie spread too much. This is counter to what we've always read. To confuse matters even more, she found the results were the opposite when subbing potato starch for tapioca starch. With the starches, it seemed, the cookies worked better when subbing by weight, not volume, although the difference is negligible either way.

Here's what we believe. Conventional wisdom will tell you to substitute one flour for another by weight. What we've found in our kitchens is that you should only sub the starches by weight. Flours should be subbed by volume and so should all-purpose mixes. You should test this out in your own kitchen and see what *you* find! Take a favorite recipe and sub in a different flour by weight. Then sub in that same flour by volume, and see which recipe turns out better. We know what happened in our kitchens. We'd love to know what happens in yours.

Recommended Brands:
- OXO
- Escali

How to convert a recipe to gluten-free:

If you do an Internet search, you'll find a variety of suggestions. We've learned that each baker has his or her own way of starting this process. We like to do one of two things. Either:

> Make your own gluten-free flour blend (directions on how to do this to follow) or use an all-purpose flour blend to start, add ½ teaspoon xanthan gum per cup of flour, and substitute it cup for cup with wheat flour. Once you see how that turns out, you can begin making changes based on your results.

or

> Almost everything you could want gluten-free has been made by someone already. Find a recipe from a source you trust, and start with that. Then make substitutions based on your desired ingredients, texture and flavor.

How to make a gluten-free flour blend:

Sift together:
1 cup flour (any flour you like) +
1 cup flour (any other flour you like) +
1 cup starch (your preference of starch)

---

3 cups all-purpose mix

You can use any two types of flour (except almond, cassava or potato flour) for this.

How to make gluten-free yeast breads:

Gluten-free yeast breads are the most challenging aspect of gluten-free baking. Who hasn't heard horror stories about gluten-free bread that turned out as hard as a doorstop? This challenge scared us more than any other in this project but we were determined to conquer it. After hundreds of trials and a few headaches, we finally understand the basics of gluten-free yeast bread. There are a number of yeasted bread recipes in these guides that you will love.

Here are some of our tips:

- Gluten-free yeast breads are not like yeast breads made with gluten. One difference is the kneading process. There are very few gluten-free recipes that will call for kneading. Generally we prefer to use a hand or stand mixer to do the kneading for us.

- Gluten-free breads only need to rise once whereas wheat-based breads need to rise several times. Thus, the preparation for gluten-free yeast breads takes less time.

- Xanthan gum and gum replacements like whole psyllium husks are very important in creating structure in bread recipes. In a round of experimentation for our Artisan Sandwich Bread, we tried using ¼ teaspoon less of xanthan gum and our bread lost 4 full inches of height!

- Focus on the protein. Protein gives yeast breads the structure they require. We had great success when we combined a bean flour with superfine rice flour and potato starch. Other high protein flours can yield great results as well.

- Eggs are a gluten-free bread's best friend. We like to beat our eggs heavily in our recipes to add some extra volume. We also like to add stiff egg whites to our bread batters.

- Superfine flours are recommended for gluten-free bread because they help the bread poof up higher. These superfine flours have a smaller grain size and therefore are lighter in weight. This allows the yeast to spring up. Heavy grainy flours weigh the loaf down.

- Gluten-free yeast breads require more liquid. If there's not enough liquid, the flour will weigh the dough down and it will not rise. Too much liquid will cause your bread to rise too much. It will become a "poufy bread monster" with giant air pockets and it may also collapse.

- In most cases gluten-free breads need to be made in a pan to give them the proper shape. Since their batter is runny, they will spread rather than rise without the support.

- Gluten-filled recipes rise easily. You stick them on the stove and they just grow. This is not always the case with gluten-free. We give our gluten-free breads a fighting chance to rise by using specific proofing methods. Proofing the dough in a warm moist location makes all the difference in the world. Here are our favorite methods:

Best Methods for Proofing Your Dough (*a.k.a.* how to make a steam box):

1. Our #1 method for getting your dough to rise is to make a steam box in your microwave. Put two microwave-safe jars filled with water in the microwave and turn it on for about 15-20 minutes. Prepare bread dough while you wait. When the dough is ready to rise, quickly open the microwave and stick your bowl of dough inside. Shut it quickly so the steam doesn't escape. Let rise for the duration as per the instructions. Note: Opening the microwave door to check on the bread causes the needed steam to escape. Don't let your curiosity get the best of you!

2. If you don't have a microwave or your recipe calls for the dough to be shaped before rising (such as with our Soft Pretzels recipe), make a steam box in your oven. Turn the oven on to the lowest heat. Then put an oven-safe bowl of water on the lowest rung. Once the oven is pre-heated, turn it off to cool while you prepare your dough. Once the dough is ready to rise, place a towel over it and place it into the oven. Allow the bread to rise for the required time.

3. A third method that works surprisingly well is the stove-top method. Put your dough into a large skillet. Put the top on the skillet and turn the burner on low for 2 minutes. Then turn it off and let the dough rise. This method traps condensation in the pan. We use this method for our English Muffins, Cheesy Skillet Biscuits and Cilantro Pesto Stuffed Rolls.

Understanding Alternative Sweeteners

Sugar is more than a sweetener when used in baked goods. It's an important ingredient that provides moisture, structure and browning when baked. There are many types of sweeteners on the market today. They come in two forms: liquid and granulated. Liquid sweeteners are, as their name implies, liquid in nature. Granulated sugars are crystallized. Many people like to substitute sugars in their recipes. It's fine to substitute, but keep in mind the texture and flavor you are trying to achieve. These will change with any substitutions. The more you experiment the better you'll understand the behavior of each sweetener.

There are a vast number of options for both liquid and granulated sweeteners on the market today. These different sugars come in a variety of price points and each offer their own health benefits. For this book we chose to use primarily the unrefined healthier varieties. One of the most common questions we are asked is how these different sugars can be exchanged in baked good recipes. It's not an easy question to answer but we've spent months experimenting and what follows are our discoveries:

Granulated Sugars
Organic Cane Sugar
White cane sugar and organic cane sugar are generally the same. The glycemic index is lower in organic cane sugar and it tends to be coarser.

We have successfully replaced them cup for cup. Most of our recipes call for the use of unrefined granulated sugar. In most of these recipes regular inexpensive table sugar will work, unless otherwise specified.

Recommended Brand:
- **Woodstock Farms Pure Cane Sugar**

Turbinado *a.k.a.* Raw Sugar:
Turbinado sugar is made from cane juice, just like sugar. It is extracted during an earlier period in the processing and retains some of the nutrients and flavor of molasses. Turbinado sugar can be used as a substitute for brown or white sugar

Pros: Many claim that turbinado sugar is healthier because it's less processed, is lower in calories than granulated sugar and contains trace amount of minerals.

Cons: Turbinado sugar undergoes processing to produce the finished product and loses most of its molasses and nutrient content. While it is lower on the glycemic index than refined table sugar, turbinado sugar does raise your blood sugar so we don't recommended it for diabetics.

Baking Tips:
- This sugar is usually very coarsely ground and is perfect sprinkled on top of baked goods or rolled into cookies.

- This coarse grind can be problematic in baked goods as it will take longer to break down in the oven. You can run the sugar through a coffee grinder or process it in your blender to create a powder. This will give your baked goods a better overall texture and allow for the sugar to do its job.

- It works well as a replacement for white granulated sugar cup for cup when it is powdered.

- It will add a very light golden color to baked goods.

Sucanat:

Sucanat is pure dried sugar cane juice. Through a mechanical process of heating and cooling the juice, small sugar grains are formed. Sucanat is generally accepted as a substitute for brown sugar.

Pros: It contains trace amount of nutrients as it is not as highly processed as white sugar. It can be used as a 1:1 replacement for refined sugar.

Cons: Although less refined, it's still sugar and is problematic for people with certain health problems, such as diabetes.

Baking Tips:

- This sugar works wonderfully as a replacement for brown sugar because of its caramel flavor. However, it contains less moisture than brown sugar since brown sugar contains molasses. To replicate brown sugar we suggest adding some molasses to your Sucanat in recipes.

- Will lend baked goods a light brown/dark golden color.

- Like many other sugars, it is coarsely ground. Please read recipe instructions carefully. Some may require you to powder the unrefined granulated sugar. If you don't, results will vary.

- Makes wonderful frosting and glazes in powdered form.

- Palm sugar can be replaced with Sucanat cup for cup, yielding extremely similar results. They provide a similar flavor and moisture level to baked goods.

- Can be used as a cup for cup replacement for white sugar in most applications. That being said, you will notice that Sucanat will add less moisture to your baked goods than regular white sugar. Exchanging the two sugars may be problematic in recipes with a sensitive moisture content (e.g. graham crackers, biscotti or fried doughnuts).

Recommended Brand:
- **Wholesome Sweeteners Organic Sucanat**

Coconut Palm Sugar:

Coconut palm sugar is made from the sap of the coconut tree. The taste is similar to brown sugar, with a sweet hint of molasses.

Pros: Coconut palm sugar has a low glycemic index. This makes it a safer choice for diabetics or anyone looking to watch their weight. It is rich in many vitamins and minerals.

Cons: Coconut palm sugar can be expensive and is not as widely available as other sweeteners.

Baking Tips

- Palm sugar works the same as Sucanat. Refer to the tips on Sucanat for how to use it.

Recommended Brands:

- **Navitas Naturals**
- **Big Tree Farms: In addition to regular coconut palm sugar, Big Tree Farms has palm sugar that has been infused with other flavors: ginger, turmeric, and vanilla. These are good additions to both sweet and savory baked goods.**

Maple Sugar:

As the name implies, maple sugar is made from the syrup that comes from maple trees. Often made into tasty maple candy, it can also be turned into a sugar for baking.

Pros: This is often considered a more natural choice than sugar. It is sweeter than sugar, thus less will be needed in baking applications.

Cons: It is high on the glycemic index and is expensive and difficult to find.

Baking Tips:

- Substitute ⅔ cup of maple sugar for every 1 cup of granulated sugar in your recipes.
- Wonderful for streusel toppings.

Recommended Brand:

- **Shiloh Farms**

Date Sugar:

Date sugar is a natural sweetener produced by powdering or grinding dehydrated dates. It is light brown in color, has a very sweet taste, and a grainy texture.

Pros: Can be used in baking where the recipe does not require melting of sugar. One cup of refined sugar can be replaced by about two-thirds cup of date sugar. It's a better source of vitamins and minerals than refined table sugar.

Cons: Dates are high on the glycemic index is not recommended for diabetics.

Baking Tips:

- Use in a 1:1 ratio for granulated sugar.
- Delicious sweetener to use in raw recipes, like raw cheesecakes.
- Can be used to create a crunchy texture when rolled into cookies.
- Run this sugar through your coffee grinder or in your blender to create a finely ground powdered sugar. It will work great in frosting recipes.
- Date sugar will add a brown tint to the applications where it is added.

Recommended Brand:

- **Shiloh Farms**

Stevia:

Stevia extract comes from the plant of the same name, also known as stevia rebaudiana. You can grow the plant just as you would any other herb and mince it for use in cooking or teas.

Pros: Stevia does not raise blood sugar and has zero calories. It is a suitable option for diabetics or anyone watching their weight or blood sugar.

Cons: Many brands of stevia have a strong aftertaste and it is expensive. However, a little goes a long way so your bottle will last for a long time. We chose not to use stevia recipes in this book because it is an acquired taste and many people do not like it. However, we both use stevia and you can find stevia-sweetened recipes on our blogs.

Baking Tips:

Note that when we talk about baking with stevia, we're talking about the liquid or crystal extracts that are made up only of stevia. You can buy stevia products that have fillers in them to make it easier to use cup for cup as a substitute for sugar.

- Stevia cannot be used cup for cup in baked good recipes.

- Stevia is especially effective when used in conjunction with small amounts of honey or other natural sugars. It increases their sweetness exponentially so that less sugar may be used in a recipe.

- A little bit goes a long way. Using too much will create an unappealing aftertaste.

- About ⅓-½ teaspoon of powdered stevia (depending on the brand) = 1 cup of sugar.

- ½ teaspoon liquid stevia = 1 cup of sugar.

- Baked goods often depend on sugar to provide structure and moisture. It will take a ton of experimentation to produce a decent baked good that relies only on stevia and no other sweeteners. We look to replace the same volume of sugar with pureed fruit, ground nuts or seeds, finely ground coconut flakes, certified gluten-free rolled oats, and quinoa flakes. All of these will change the result of your baked good. We encourage you to experiment!

- Add extra salt when working with stevia. The salt will help balance the flavor.

- Stevia is an acquired taste. If you need to use stevia for health reasons, try cutting out all other sugar for a few weeks. It will help your palate become accustomed to the flavor and aftertaste.

Recommended Brands:
- **NuNaturals stevia far surpasses the other brands. Their products do not carry a strong bitter aftertaste. We especially love their Liquid Vanilla Stevia.**
- **Sweetleaf is second only to NuNaturals in flavor.**

Xylitol:

Xylitol is a natural sugar alcohol sweetener. It can be used in most recipes that call for refined cane sugar.

Pros: Xylitol has the same sweetness as sugar, but contains fewer calories and is significantly lower on the glycemic index. It is often touted as an alternative sweetener for individuals dealing with candida. It is used in gum because it is less likely to cause tooth decay than sugar.

Cons: Can cause stomach discomfort if eaten in excess.

Baking Tips:

- Xylitol, in most cases, can be exchanged for refined table sugar cup for cup in recipes.

- We noticed one very unique characteristic of xylitol: When we removed our recipes from the oven, they were often too moist. However, twenty-four hours later, that same baked good developed the perfect moisture level. Therefore, we recommend when you use xylitol to plan a day ahead. Once your baked good has cooled, cover and leave it at room temperature for a day.

- Xylitol may change the texture of your baked goods. We noticed it had a tendency to add a gummy texture to a few of our cookie recipes.

- Xylitol has a bit of an artificial flavor if used in excess. Baking usually hides this flavor but if you notice it, simply back off of the amount used.

- Xylitol can be used to make sugar-free powdered sugar. Due to its strong flavor, we suggest combining it with other strong flavors to make frostings.

- Xylitol is not recommended in recipes containing yeast.

Erythritol Crystals:

Erythritol is a sugar alcohol found naturally in fruits and some fermented foods. Like xylitol, it won't cause tooth decay. Our knowledge and experience with this sugar is limited. We do not recommend the use of this sugar in our baked goods as we did not test it in all of the recipes. If you prefer to use it, here's what we know:

Pros: It does not cause blood sugar spikes like sugar does.

Cons: It is generally derived from corn, which many are sensitive to.

Baking Tips:

- In most cases, erythritol can be used cup for cup in baking applications but this amount may need be to be adjusted as it is less sweet than sugar.

- We noticed that this sugar attributed much less moisture in our baked goods.

- Erythritol is white in color and will not change the color of your baked goods.

Liquid Sugars

Honey:

There is a big difference between raw honey, which you can often find locally, and the processed honey you find at the grocery store. The former is a natural sweetener full of vitamins and minerals. The latter is devoid of nutritional value and may contain high fructose corn syrup.

Pros: Raw honey, as noted, is a nutritional powerhouse and is considered one of nature's superfoods. It is much lower on the glycemic index than sugar or highly processed honey.

Cons: Raw, local honey is often expensive. Honey should not be given to infants.

Baking Tips:

- For every cup of granulated sugar, use ¾ cup of honey. Reduce the liquid ingredients by 2 tablespoons, and you may need to add ¼ teaspoon of baking soda to reduce the acidity of the honey.

- Honey can make some gluten-free baked goods too chewy. We experienced this in a few of our muffin recipes when we tried replacing maple syrup with honey. Replacing sugar with honey in crispy recipes may result in a softer product.

- Honey is extremely sweet, therefore less is usually needed in most recipes.

Recommended Brand:

- **Big Tree Farms has a variety of flavors of honey.**

Brown Rice Syrup:

Brown rice syrup is derived from cooked rice that has been broken down by enzymes. The liquid is strained and cooked down to a thick consistency. Brown rice syrup is thicker than many other liquid sweeteners.

Pros: Brown rice syrup breaks down in the body slower than sugar and will not cause as intense of a blood sugar spike.

Cons: Brown rice syrup is slightly lower than sugar on the glycemic index, thus it is not the best option for diabetics. Some

brands contain barley and therefore are not gluten-free. It is important to read the ingredients list carefully.

Baking Tips:

- Its mild flavor works well in most baking applications.

- Can be used as a replacement for honey, agave nectar and maple syrup, although each will impart a slightly unique flavor.

- For every cup of granulated sugar, you can replace with 1¼ cups of brown rice syrup, reducing another liquid in the recipe by ¼ cup.

Recommended Brand:

- **Lundberg Family Farms**

Coconut Nectar:

Coconut nectar is similar to coconut palm sugar. It is lower on the glycemic index than sugar, and is often used in raw food recipes.

Pros: Coconut nectar is low glycemic and nutrient dense.

Cons: It is expensive and not everyone loves the mild flavor. Due to its high cost, we have experimented very little with this sweetener and can only offer a few tips.

Baking Tips:

- Can be used as a replacement for honey in baked goods, but has a milder flavor. For those with a strong sweet tooth, this might not be the best sweetener. However, for those of you who don't need your cookies to be super sweet, this is a great option!

- Use a 1:1 ratio when replacing other liquid sweeteners.

Recommended Brand:
- **Big Tree Farms**

Maple Syrup:
Made from the sap of the maple tree, it has a delicious flavor that we love to use in our baked goods.

Pros: It has a high concentration of minerals and is sweet enough that a little goes a long way.

Cons: Like many other natural sweeteners, it is expensive. It is higher on the glycemic index than coconut nectar and is not a great option for diabetics.

Baking Tips:
- Can be used in a 1:1 ratio with other liquid sweeteners. Just remember it's very sweet and that less may be more.
- In general, you replace a cup of granulated sugar with ¾ cup of maple syrup. You may need to reduce the other liquids in the recipe by a small amount (up to 3 tablespoons).

Molasses:
Molasses is what remains behind after the processing of cane sugar. It can come in three varieties: mild, dark and blackstrap. We recommend using organic blackstrap molasses in your baking. Blackstrap molasses has a higher nutritional value compared with both regular molasses and sugar and contains iron, magnesium, zinc, calcium, copper, phosphorus, and potassium.

Pros: Blackstrap molasses is high in iron and many other vitamins and minerals. No other sweetener imparts quite the same unique flavor.

Cons: Blackstrap molasses should only be used in recipes where you want that strong flavor. It often needs to be combined with another sweetener to neutralize the bitter flavor.

Baking Tips:
- We love using molasses in conjunction with strongly flavored flours, like buckwheat.
- It tastes wonderful in breads, cookies and cakes.
- Often works best when combined with another sweetener.
- Will add a dark rich color to baked goods.

Recommended Brand:
- **Plantation Unsulphured Blackstrap Molasses**

Agave Nectar:
Agave nectar is a hot topic of debate these days. While it was originally recommended for diabetics due to being low on the glycemic index, recent research suggests that it may be no better for you than high fructose corn syrup. Due to this controversy and lack of strong evidence either way, we tend to avoid it in our baking. It can be found in light, dark, amber and raw varieties, each of which will give your baked goods a slightly different flavor.

Pros: Agave nectar is lower on the glycemic index than refined sugar. It is also very sweet so you can often use less in your recipes than you might with other sweeteners.

Cons: The ultimate safety of commercial agave nectar is under debate and we recommend individuals do their own research. The quality of the brand is extremely important and there are many low quality brands on the market. If using it, we recommend you buy an organic brand that you trust.

Baking Tips:

- Most brands of agave work well to make candy, which usually requires a high temperature. We have used it to make caramel, toffee and more.

- Agave is thinner than some of the other liquid sweeteners.

- Agave has a sweet but neutral flavor that works well in most recipes.

- Can be used as a replacement for honey in most baked goods. The neutral flavor will not change the overall integrity of your recipe.

Recommended Brands:
- Madhava
- Wholesome Sweeteners

Yacon Syrup:

Yacon syrup comes from the South American tuber of the same name. It is similar in flavor to molasses, and is a good low-glycemic option.

Pros: A good option for diabetics and those on an anti-candida diet.

Cons: Once again, like other natural sweeteners, it is expensive and not often found in regular grocery stores.

Baking Tips:
- Use in a 1:1 ratio as a substitute for molasses.

Recommended Brand:
- Navitas Naturals

You don't like using xanthan gum in your recipes? Here's how to replace it:

- **Guar Gum:** Use an equal amount of guar gum. The two work almost exactly the same, and we have not noticed a difference in our recipes based on which we used. Guar gum is often preferred by individuals with sensitivities to corn.

- **1 tablespoon ground flax seed meal + 1 tablespoon ground chia seeds (or whole psyllium husks) + 6 tablespoons boiling water (or room temperature full-fat canned coconut milk):** Flax, chia, and psyllium all have incredible binding properties. By mixing 1 tablespoon of ground flax seed meal with 3 tablespoons of hot or boiling water, you'll end up with an "egg" that helps bind your ingredients together and replace an actual egg. This is usually mixed in with the wet ingredients after it has had a few minutes to form a gel. But one flax egg usually isn't enough to bind entire recipes together. You often need to add another egg made with ground chia or whole psyllium husks.

There are a number of methods for using these ingredients to replace xanthan gum. In our recipes, we have specified which ones worked equally well with psyllium husks or chia seeds. If the recipe does not specify that you can use either, it is best to only use the ingredient specified. In some cases, the two cannot be used interchangeably.

Recommended Brands:
- **Flax Seeds: Navitas Naturals, Shiloh Farms**
- **Chia Seeds: Navitas Naturals, Shiloh Farms**
- **Whole Psyllium Husks: Yerba Prima**

The bigger your baked good is the more help it will need to hold it together. Something like a cookie might be able to get away with just one flax egg, half a flax egg or may not even need one.

In recipes like cakes, a full tablespoon each of flax and chia or flax and psyllium is needed. In that case, you'll need a total of 6 tablespoons of boiling water. Bread recipes require even more and in that case we often use up to ¼ cup of psyllium husks in some recipes. You will need to rely on experimentation here, as this is not an exact science. This process will make your recipes moister and fluffier but may not be your desired result.

If you're making a recipe that requires cold ingredients like our Buttermilk Biscuits or Curry Scones, you can use room temperature full-fat canned coconut milk instead of boiling water.

Replacing Common Ingredients

How to replace dairy:

To replace 1 cup butter: Fat has a number of functions in baked goods. It can help add flavor, leaven batters, contribute flakiness and tenderness, and prevent sticking. According to its purpose and considering differing melting points, you'll want to choose the following option that best fits the baked goods you're making:

- **1 cup Earth Balance Buttery Spread (Soy Free option available):** All of our recipes that call for butter have been tested with Earth Balance Soy-Free Buttery Spread. We do not recommend using other types of margarine as our testers reported disastrous results.

- **1 cup shortening (Spectrum Organic Palm Shortening is soy free):** Shortening can generally be used to replace butter, but you'll lose some of that delicious buttery flavor. For recipes in our book that call for shortening, it's best to stick with that as the other options have lower melting points. If a cookie recipe calls for shortening and you use butter, Earth Balance, coconut oil, or oil, it will likely spread too quickly and make a large, flat cookie.

- **1 cup coconut oil:** This is a great substitute for butter. Coconut oil's melting point is slightly lower than butter, but in general, this is a good allergen-free replacement.

Recommended Brand:
- Garden of Life

- **1 cup oil:** When melted butter is called for in a recipe, any mild flavored oil, such as canola, grapeseed, extra light olive oil, or melted coconut oil can be used. However, in recipes where you cream the butter, you cannot use an oil. The process of creaming the butter creates air pockets that help create tender, flaky baked goods. Oil will not offer this structure.

- **Applesauce:** To reduce the amount of fat in a recipe, you can sub in applesauce or other pureed fruits. Start with a smaller amount (replace ¼ cup of the fat with ¼ cup of applesauce), and increase as you like. Baked goods made with applesauce will be more moist, less flaky and may require a longer baking time.

To replace 1 cup milk: A quick note for those that can eat dairy products. Keep the following rule in mind when baking with dairy. Fat creates tenderness and moisture. The higher the fat content, usually the better the baked good. The options are:

- **1 cup full-fat canned coconut milk:** Our all time favorite milk to bake with is coconut milk. The high fat content gives a very rich result.

Recommended Brand:
- We found that Thai Kitchen contains more cream than any other brand. However, Native Forest coconut milk contains only traces of BPA in its can, while other brands may contain more.

- **1 cup almond, hemp, or soy milk:** These higher-protein milks help add structure to your recipe. This will aid in helping your baked good rise without collapsing.

- **1 cup rice milk, water, or fruit juice:** These substitutes are more like the equivalent of adding fat-free milk, but without the protein. Depending on the flavor profile you're looking for, all of these options are effective. It can be fun to replace milk with juice in white cakes for a new flavor.

To replace 1 cup buttermilk: Buttermilk is a cultured dairy product that adds moisture and tanginess to your baked goods. When buttermilk is heated, the bacteria in it convert a portion of the milk's sugar into acid. Acid is the ingredient for success. Acid will make your baking powder and baking soda *thrive*. To make your own:

- Mix 1 cup of the milk (any variety, dairy or nondairy) + 1 tablespoon of lemon juice, apple cider vinegar, or 1¾ teaspoons of cream of tartar. Stir together and set aside for a few minutes until it begins to curdle.

To replace heavy cream in recipes: Heavy (Full-Fat) Canned Coconut Milk. This works cup for cup in the place of heavy cream in baked goods.

Recommended Brands:
- Thai Kitchen
- Native Forest

To replace 1 cup cream cheese or sour cream: There are a variety of soy cream cheeses and sour creams on the market. For those who don't use soy or prefer to make your own, here's what we like to do:

- Cashew cream cheese/sour cream: To make approximately 1 cup of cream cheese, soak 1½ cups raw cashews in water for at least 4 hours. Rinse and drain, then puree in a food processor along with ¾ teaspoon apple cider vinegar, 1½ teaspoons lemon juice, and ¼ teaspoon salt. Add milk 1 teaspoon at a time until desired consistency is reached.

To replace 1 cup yogurt:
- 1 cup unsweetened applesauce or other fruit puree
- 1 cup non-dairy yogurt
- 1 cup cashew sour cream, thinned to the desired consistency with milk

Avoiding Dairy in Chocolate:

Most brands of chocolate chips are made with dairy. We love Enjoy Life Foods Chocolate Chips and Chocolate Chunks as they are free of gluten, dairy and soy.

How to replace eggs:

Eggs work wonders in gluten-free recipes. We love using them because they work as binders, leaveners, and also help your baked goods dry inside. This can create a light and fluffy cake that won't fall apart. However, there are many of us that can't or choose not to eat eggs. There are many options for replacing eggs:

To mimic the binding properties of egg try any of the following:

Flax, Chia or Psyllium Egg: Replace 1 egg with 1 tablespoon of ground flax seed meal, ground chia seeds, or whole psyllium husks. Stir in 3 tablespoons of boiling water and let sit. For flax and chia seed meal, you can let it sit longer, but psyllium will congeal too much, so you want to stir and then add it to your wet ingredients immediately. This option helps bind ingredients together, which is why we also use this substitution for xanthan gum, as described earlier. Because this will not provide the leavening properties of eggs, you can add a small amount of baking powder if you want a better rise (½ teaspoon).

Tapioca Gel: To keep your recipes from crumbling, you can also use 1 tablespoon tapioca starch mixed with ¼ cup of warm water

Applesauce: 4 tablespoons of unsweetened applesauce, fruit puree, or pureed white or garbanzo beans plus 1 teaspoon baking powder. This will make recipes more moist than an egg will, so adjust your baking time as needed.

Ener-G Egg Replacer: Follow the directions on the box.

To mimic just the leavening properties of egg (make things rise):

- 1 teaspoon baking powder + 1 tablespoon water + 1 tablespoon apple cider vinegar

- To mimic egg whites, which create an incredible rise:

It is not recommended to replace more than 2 egg whites in a recipe. Some recipes, like our Gingerbread Angelfood Cake, are impossible to make without eggs.

Agar agar: Mix 1 tablespoon agar agar powder (not the flakes) into 1 tablespoon of water. Beat, put in the fridge for 15 minutes, then beat again before using in your recipe.

Eggs have a magical ability to deal with high levels of fat in recipes. For example, our Flaky Pie Crust and Nilla-Style Wafers depend on eggs for their texture. Removing the eggs will make both of these recipes extremely gummy. In gluten-free baking we suggest you avoid removing eggs from high fat recipes such as these.

How to replace corn:

We do not use cornstarch in our baking. However, we do use xanthan gum, which is often derived from corn. This can be easily replaced using our suggestions as noted earlier. Believe it or not, baking powder may also contain corn. Hain's featherlight baking powder is corn free. You can also make your own baking powder:

Baking Powder Recipe: to make 1 tablespoon of baking powder, combine:

> 1 teaspoon baking soda + 2 teaspoons cream of tartar + 1 teaspoon tapioca or arrowroot starch. Use immediately.

Vanilla Extract: Our favorite brand of pure vanilla extract is Simply Organic Pure Vanilla Extract. It is derived from corn, but according to the company, the distillation process makes it corn free. However, some brands can contain corn and making your own is easy!

> Combine 6 vanilla beans and 2 cups of vodka into a sealed container. Store in a dark space for 2 months, shaking every so often. After the 2 months, use vanilla extract in all your recipes! Vanilla beans can be re-used to make a second and third batch.

Powdered Sugar: Many commercial brands of powdered sugar can contain corn. Trader Joe's is an exception. You can make your own powdered sugar using our recipe in the frosting section.

Earth Balance products can contain corn. Read our dairy substitution section for alternatives to butter and Earth Balance.

Ask the Expert

Katie Higgins is better known as Chocolate Covered Katie, the name of her popular vegan recipe blog. While not a gluten-free baker, she occasionally likes to develop gluten-free recipes. From cupcakes to brownies and cookies, she knows how to play around with ingredients in unusual ways. We've asked her to share her experiences with gluten-free baking and substituting ingredients.

Do you remember the first thing you ever baked gluten-free? How did it turn out? The first thing I ever baked to be specifically gluten-free was Breakfast Pizza. I'd heard about coconut flour, and I love all things coconut. So I was excited to try it out. But I'd also heard that you shouldn't use just coconut flour for baking, because it would yield a crumbly result. So I bought garbanzo bean flour for the recipe as well. It was delicious! I posted the recipe on my blog, and others love it, too, even people who aren't gluten-free!

What kind of gluten-free recipes would you suggest for a beginner to start with? My deep-dish cookie pie is a huge hit and easy to make, too. I'd recommend it for beginners because they probably have all the ingredients on hand (or they don't need to go to a specialty store to find the ingredients). It doesn't call for any flour at all, and it doesn't call for xanthan/guar gum. Plus it shows people that gluten-free baked goods can taste delicious and gooey, not crumbly and dry.

When you get an idea in mind for a certain recipe, do you usually start with a non-vegan recipe and convert it, or start with a vegan recipe? When baking, I usually look at non-vegan recipes before starting out. But since I'll be substituting so many things (eggs, butter, milk), I don't actually use the non-vegan recipes as anything more than a guideline for the types of ingredients to include.

What do you generally use as egg replacers in baking? I am a big fan of Ener-g Egg Replacer. Applesauce works great as a binder, and I've just started to experiment with flax as an egg replacer.

What so you do when you want to get a baked good to rise more? I often use baking powder if I want a baked good to rise more.

What kind of dairy-free replacements do you like to bake with? Do you think the changes affect the texture and flavor? My favorite dairy-free replacement is Almond Breeze almond milk. I adore it! I also use dairy-free chocolate chips and I don't think they taste any different from how I remember chocolate-chips with dairy to taste. There are so many amazing vegan products on the market now that taste almost exactly like their dairy counterparts (or better!).

You use a variety of sweeteners in your baked goods? What are your favorites to work with and why? My favorite sweetener is probably NuNaturals stevia. I've found that this one has the least-offensive aftertaste of all the stevia brands and it doesn't leave me feeling sluggish like sugar does. However, it's a tightrope walk when baking with sweeteners, because you have to find the balance between what's healthier (stevia) and what tastes better and yields a better texture (sugar).

Another favorite sweetener is over-ripe banana. It's amazing how you can use bananas to sweeten foods like oatmeal or even chocolate pie. I have a Raw Chocolate Fudge Cake recipe on my blog that is sweetened only with banana, and it's one of my blog's most-popular recipes.

What is your favorite cream cheese alternative for baking? Tofutti (non-hydrogenated) is my favorite cream cheese sub.

What is your favorite sour cream alternative for baking? I sometimes use Mori-Nu tofu and lemon in my recipes, so I guess you could call this a sour cream substitute.

What is your favorite buttermilk alternative for baking? Almond milk or soy milk curdled with vinegar.

What type of starch do you use when needed in a recipe (cornstarch, potato starch, tapioca starch, arrowroot starch)? How do you decide which one to use? I usually use arrowroot for cooking, but when I am making a recipe for the blog I usually use cornstarch because I know it's what most people will have.

Is there anything else you think our readers should know about vegan or gluten-free baking? Don't think of it as crazy or gross. Many normal recipes are actually already vegan: sorbet, fruit crisps, PB&J's, etc. Vegan baking isn't as weird as it might sound! The same goes for gluten-free; sometimes I'll make a recipe and only realize it's gluten-free after I've made it!

Chapter 2

Almond Flour

. . . .

Almond flour is a gluten-free baking superstar, and is one of our absolute favorites. It's no wonder the use of this extraordinary flour has become abundantly popular. While many gluten-free flours have their limitations, almond flour is different. It works extremely well on its own in most cookie, cake and pastry recipes. This allows for fewer ingredients in the recipe, which is always a good thing! Almond flour is also a good source of protein and healthy fats, and is low in carbohydrates, making it a favorite for those watching their carb intake. The naturally occurring nutty and slightly sweet flavor will help you to reduce the amount of sweetener a recipe requires. If you don't have an allergy or sensitivity to nuts, we recommend keeping your fridge stocked with this versatile flour.

When we first began working with almond flour, none of our recipes turned out. We've included a list of the tips we gathered along the way. We suggest you begin with our recipes before experimenting on your own. Once you get a knack for it, you can begin your own recipe development utilizing our tips.

Nutritional Highlights:

High in protein and heart healthy fats, almond flour recipes will give you a sense of satiety faster than many other types of flour recipes. It's also low in carbohydrates, making it a good low-glycemic option.

Brand Comparison:

Almond flour can be blanched (skins removed and ground) or unblanched (almonds are ground with skins intact). We recommend using only blanched almond flour for the recipes in this book as it is less coarse than unblanched. You also want to make sure you're buying a brand that is finely ground. When it's not finely ground it will have less ability to absorb moisture, which will often alter the intended result of the recipe. We've tested the following brands. You can get better deals by purchasing the flour online than from store shelves.

- **Honeyville Blanched Almond Flour**
- **Nuts.com**
- **JK Gourmet**

Bob's Red Mill: (www.bobsredmill.com)

Bob's Red Mill almond flour is often the only brand found in grocery stores. It is coarser than many other brands and the results will not be as light or airy. Whenever you use this flour in the place of blanched almond flour, you risk the chance that the recipe will not work. We recommend this flour in applications that would use finely chopped almonds such as piecrusts or toppings. That said, the recipe testers confirmed that our Magic Bars, Italian-Style Flatbread, Orange Poppyseed

Scones and Old-Fashioned Molasses Cookies work well with Bob's Red Mill blanched almond flour.

Best Flours to Substitute for Almond Flour:

It's best to make substitutions for almond flour only with other nut and seed flours as they have a similar chemistry. We absolutely love the extensive variety of nut and seed flours from Nuts.com. We *do not* recommend substituting any of the other flours in our books for almond flour.

Almond Flour Tips:

- Almond flour recipes do not require as much liquid or fat as other recipes. Tip: Test a small portion of whatever you are making to see what happens when cooked/baked. Adjust the liquid content to meet your intended results before baking the rest of the batch. A little bit of both fat and liquid will go a long way.

- Almond flour is slightly sweet so you can get away with using fewer sweeteners in your baked goods.

- Pancake, muffin and cake batters that are made exclusively with almond flour tend to be thin and runny.

- Recipes that use almond flour exclusively (without other flours or starches) often do not need any binders (i.e. xanthan gum). Try starting your recipe without any binders, and only add them if you find your baked good crumbling.

- When baking with almond flour, be careful not to bake anything at high temperatures for long periods of time. Almond flour has the tendency to brown quicker than other gluten-free flours due to its high fat content, so keep an eye on your baked goods and cover them with aluminum foil as needed.

- Because of its low carbohydrate content, almond flour *on its own* is not a suitable flour for yeast recipes. If you want to make something with yeast, another gluten-free flour or starch will be needed to help it rise. On the other hand, almond flour is a terrific ingredient to add to yeasted bread recipes that contain grains and starches. The protein in the almonds will help give structure to the bread.

- Almond flour loves eggs. The eggs help the flour rise and hold together. Eggs can help to lighten baked goods since almond flour tends to be a little heavy on its own. However, with some creativity, you can bake without eggs. The addition of light starches and flours will help give the baked good the "lift" you intend.

- Converting an almond flour recipe to a coconut flour or other gluten-free flour recipe (and vice versa) will often require a number of modifications. Almond flour uses significantly less fat and liquid, and it takes a lot of trial and error to figure out the difference.

Store your almond flour in the fridge or freezer in an airtight container. If you use it regularly, the fridge is fine. Otherwise, store in the freezer and allow it to come to room temperature before baking.

Fun uses for almond flour

- Can be used as breading for most baking and frying applications.
- Can be used to thicken sauces. Heat the sauce in a pan over low heat. Gradually add small amounts of almond flour and stir until the sauce reaches the desired consistency. This can be a handy trick when making fruit sauces for pies and other desserts (great low-carb alternative to using starches and other flours). It can even thicken a pot of soup!

Italian-Style Flatbread

··

This flatbread is soft on the inside with a crunchy exterior. It can be sliced thin and served with hummus or cut into panini-size slices to make sandwiches. We like to use sea salt in this recipe, but regular table salt will work just fine. If you're in the mood for something sweet, skip the savory filling and sprinkle it with cinnamon and sugar before baking.

Yield: One 12 x 14 inch rectangle

DIRECTIONS:

1. Preheat oven to 400 degrees F. Grease a cookie sheet (approximately 12 x 14 inches) and set aside.

2. Heat 2 teaspoons of olive oil in a small skillet over medium-low heat. Add onions and sauté until just tender, 3-4 minutes. Add garlic and continue to sauté for about 1 minute, stirring constantly. Take off heat and put in a small bowl. Stir in basil, olives, and sun-dried tomatoes. Set aside.

3. In a large bowl, whisk almond flour, tapioca starch, xanthan gum, baking powder, and salt with a fork.

4. In a medium-sized bowl, whisk water and ¼ cup of oil. Pour into dry ingredients, stirring constantly until evenly mixed.

5. Stir in the onion, garlic, basil, olives, and sun-dried tomatoes.

6. Spoon the dough onto the middle of the cookie sheet. With the back of a spoon, spread the dough until it almost reaches all four corners of the sheet. It should be about an inch thick, but no more. It will be really sticky, but this is how it should be! Brush olive oil on the dough and sprinkle lightly with ⅛ teaspoon of fine grain sea salt. Bake for 30-35 minutes, until it begins to get golden brown on top.

7. Let cool, then cut into slices. You can cut larger slices to use as sandwich bread or smaller slices to use as dipping bread.

The bread is best when eaten fresh from the oven, but leftovers can be stored in an airtight container in the fridge for days or frozen for later use.

INGREDIENTS:

2 teaspoons olive oil

¼ medium onion, diced (approximately ½ cup)

2 cloves garlic, minced

¼ cup packed fresh basil, minced

¼ cup pitted Kalamata olives, chopped (optional)

¼ cup sun-dried tomatoes, diced

178 grams blanched almond flour (1½ lightly filled cups plus 3 tablespoons)

112 grams tapioca starch (¾ cup plus 3 tablespoons)

2½ teaspoons xanthan gum

4 teaspoons baking powder

½ teaspoon fine grain sea salt plus ⅛ teaspoon extra for sprinkling

1½ cups water

¼ cup olive oil

Zucchini Bread

INGREDIENTS:

250 grams blanched almond flour (2¼ packed cups)

255 grams potato starch (1½ cups)

30 grams flax seed meal (¼ cup)

1¼ teaspoons xanthan gum

½ teaspoon salt

1 teaspoon baking soda

1 teaspoon baking powder

2 large eggs

⅓ cup unsweetened applesauce

⅓ cup mild flavored oil or melted butter

2 teaspoons pure vanilla extract

¾ cup granulated sugar

1 teaspoon ground cinnamon

1 teaspoon ground nutmeg

1 teaspoon lemon juice (or apple cider vinegar)

2 cups grated zucchini

There is an undeniable comfort that comes from a slice of buttered zucchini bread with a cup of steaming hot coffee. We think this loaf is a little extra special. The combination of almond flour and flax meal create a texture and flavor that will capture your taste buds. Not in the mood for zucchini? Try substituting in other grated vegetables or fruits.

Yield: One 9-inch loaf

DIRECTIONS:

1. Preheat oven to 325 degrees F. Grease a 9-inch loaf pan and set aside.

2. In the bowl of a stand mixer, combine all ingredients except for the zucchini, adding the lemon juice last. Mix on medium speed until the batter comes together.

3. Stir in the zucchini by hand.

4. Quickly pour batter into the greased loaf pan and bake for 60 minutes or until a toothpick comes out clean. Remove from oven and allow to cool before slicing.

Store in an airtight container at room temperature or freeze for later use.

Blackberry & Lime Cobbler

Blackberries and lime are a match made in heaven. They are one of our all time favorite flavor combinations! For those looking for a more classic cobbler, any fruit filling will work with this delicious and quick biscuit topping. If you like to booze it up, try adding your favorite alcohol in place of the water called for in the filling. Serve with vanilla ice cream.

Yield: One pie or 4-5 ramekins

DIRECTIONS:

1. Preheat oven to 350 degrees F.

2. Toss prepared fruit, sugar, lime juice, water or alcohol, and tapioca starch together. Place in baking dish of your choice (you can use a pie dish or separate into individual ramekins).

3. In a large bowl, combine the almond flour, baking powder, salt, and sugar. Cut in the butter (or just stir in melted coconut oil). Add the lime juice, zest and the egg. Gently stir so that the dough comes together.

4. Plop spoonfuls of the dough onto the fruit (the cobbler will spread as it bakes). Place in oven and bake 20-25 minutes (until fruit is bubbly and cobbler is golden brown).

Store leftovers in the fridge covered.

INGREDIENTS:

FRUIT FILLING:

4-6 cups cleaned blackberries

½-¾ cup granulated sugar (any variety)

1 tablespoon lime juice

¼ cup water or alcohol of choice

2 tablespoons tapioca starch (or arrowroot starch)

COBBLER TOPPING:

262 grams blanched almond flour (2 packed cups)

2½ teaspoons baking powder

¼ teaspoon salt

½ cup granulated sugar (any variety)

2 tablespoons butter or melted coconut oil

1 teaspoon lime juice

Zest of 1 lime

1 large egg

Orange Poppyseed Scones

These scones are fast to make. The combination of almond flour and potato starch creates an outstanding biscuit-like texture. Vary the flavor by swapping out the orange extract for lemon, vanilla, raspberry or whatever else strikes your fancy. Any unrefined granulated sugar will work here. We especially loved them using xylitol.

Yield: One dozen scones

Directions:

1. Preheat oven to 400 degrees F. Set aside a cookie sheet.

2. Combine blanched almond flour, potato starch, sugar, baking soda, salt, xanthan gum, and poppyseeds in a large bowl. Cut butter in until it's in pea sized pieces.

3. In a small bowl whisk together the orange extract, egg, and zest. Pour into the large bowl, and mix together to create a crumbly dough.

4. Divide the dough into two mounds. Flatten and shape dough into circular discs and then cut into 6 pieces each (like you would a pizza.)

5. Place on a cookie sheet and bake for 11 minutes. Remove from oven and allow to cool slightly before eating.

These do not rise significantly; keep this in mind as you cut them into triangles. Store in an airtight container at room temperature or freeze for later use.

Ingredients:

145 grams blanched almond flour (1½ lightly filled cups)

170 grams potato starch (1 cup)

⅓ cup unrefined granulated sugar

¾ teaspoon baking soda

¼ teaspoon salt

1 teaspoon xanthan gum

3 tablespoons poppyseeds

⅓ cup softened butter, soft coconut oil or shortening.

2 tablespoons orange extract or oil

1 large egg

Zest of one orange

Fig Newton-Style Cookies

Not only are these cookies easy to make, but they will surprise you with their texture and flavor. They were a bit hit among our recipe testers. To simplify this recipe even further, any store bought fruit preserves can be substituted for the fig filling.

Yield: Two dozen cookies

DIRECTIONS:

1. Preheat oven to 325 degrees F.

2. Start by making the filling. In a food processor, combine figs, orange juice, and honey to taste until it becomes a thick paste. Remove and set filling aside. Clean out your food processor bowl to use again for the dough.

3. Combine blanched almond flour, potato starch, butter, agave nectar, vanilla extract, baking powder, and salt in food processor until they come together to form a smooth dough.

4. Divide dough in half. Roll half out into a narrow long rectangle (6 x 15 inches) on a sheet of parchment paper.

5. Spoon half of the filling down the center strip of dough. Using the parchment paper, gently lift and fold the two sides of dough over the center, overlapping them slightly. Wrap the dough with your parchment and gently use your hands to seal the dough, while maintaining the shape of the dough. This will help keep the filling intact and give the cookies perfect uniform shape.

6. Using a sharp knife, cut the log into 12 cookies. Place each cookie on a cookie sheet and bake for 12 minutes. Repeat with second half of dough.

Store in an airtight container at room temperature or freeze for later use.

INGREDIENTS:

FILLING:

2 cups of pitted figs, prunes or other dried fruit

5 tablespoons orange juice

Agave nectar or other liquid sweetener to taste (optional)

DOUGH:

262 grams blanched almond flour (2 packed cups)

340 grams potato starch (2 cups)

4 tablespoons butter or softened coconut oil

½ cup agave nectar (honey or any other liquid sweetener will work)

1 teaspoon pure vanilla extract

¼ teaspoon baking powder

¼ teaspoon salt

Chocolate Mint Graham Crackers

These crispy graham crackers will outshine any box of store bought crackers. Their flavor will sandwich the heck out of a marshmallow like you never knew possible. If you aren't a big fan of mint or would like some variety, try replacing the peppermint with other flavor extracts such as almond, orange, strawberry, hazelnut or vanilla.

Yield: Two dozen graham crackers

DIRECTIONS:

1. Preheat oven to 320 degrees F.

2. In the bowl of a stand mixer, mix the almond flour, potato starch, cocoa powder, sugar, baking powder, and salt.

3. Add applesauce and peppermint extract. Mix on medium-high until ingredients come together into a thick ball of dough.

4. Divide dough into two balls. Place a sheet of parchment paper (or on a non-stick mat) on a cookie sheet.

5. Roll the dough out thin on the parchment paper. Using a pizza cutter, cut the dough into squares. Gently separate so they crisp on all edges when baked. Optional: Poke holes with a fork on the surface of each cookie to resemble commercial graham crackers. Place in oven and bake for 25 minutes. Repeat with second ball of dough.

6. Allow graham crackers to cool before removing them from the cookie sheet.

Note: Finely ground brands of blanched almond flour are recommended for this recipe.

Store in an airtight container at room temperature or freeze for later use.

INGREDIENTS:

160 grams blanched almond flour (1¼ packed cups)

125 grams potato starch (¾ cup)

35 grams unsweetened cocoa powder (⅓ packed cup)

¾ cup coconut palm sugar or Sucanat

2½ teaspoons baking powder

¼ teaspoon salt

⅓ cup unsweetened applesauce

1 tablespoon peppermint extract

Molasses Spice Cookies

These soft and chewy cookies are perfect for the holidays. They remind us of our favorites from childhood. Any type of unrefined granulated sugar will work well, although we've found that we prefer coarser sugars (like turbinado sugar) for rolling the cookies in. A finer sugar like coconut palm sugar will not give the baked cookie as much texture. For variation, try making cookie sandwiches filled with our Caramel Cream Frosting.

Yield: Two dozen cookies

DIRECTIONS:

1. Whisk almond flour, brown rice flour, tapioca starch, baking powder, cinnamon, cloves, ginger, nutmeg, and salt in a large mixing bowl. Set aside.

2. In a medium-sized bowl, whisk oil, molasses, sugar, and vanilla together.

3. In a small bowl, pour boiling water over flaxseed meal and psyllium husks. Stir briefly and set aside for 1 minute. After a minute, pour this mixture into the wet ingredients and stir together.

4. Add wet ingredients to dry and stir well. Put dough in the fridge for an hour to chill.

5. After the dough has chilled, preheat the oven to 350 degrees F. Grease 2 cookie sheets.

6. Form dough into balls (1 heaping tablespoon each) and roll each ball in the sugar before placing on the cookie sheet about 2-3 tablespoons apart. Flatten slightly. Bake 11-12 minutes. Allow to cool a few minutes on the cookie sheet before moving to a cooling rack.

Store in an airtight container at room temperature or freeze for later use.

INGREDIENTS:

106 grams blanched almond flour (1 lightly filled cup)

203 grams brown rice flour (1½ lightly filled cups plus 1 tablespoon)

60 grams tapioca starch (½ cup)

2 teaspoons baking powder

¾ teaspoon ground cinnamon

½ teaspoon ground cloves

¼ teaspoon ground ginger

¼ teaspoon ground nutmeg

1 teaspoon salt

½ cup mild-flavored oil

½ cup molasses

2/3 cup unrefined granulated sugar

1 teaspoon pure vanilla extract

1 tablespoon ground flaxseed meal

1 tablespoon whole psyllium husks or ground chia seeds

5 tablespoons boiling water

¼ cup unrefined granulated sugar for rolling cookie dough

Magic Bars

· ·

Rather than the traditional graham cracker crust, we decided to go with an almond flour base for this recipe. This highlights just how simple almond flour recipes can be! The toppings are just suggestions. Try different nuts, butterscotch chips or maraschino cherries instead.

Yield: 16 bars

DIRECTIONS:

1. Preheat oven to 350 degrees F. Cut out a piece of parchment paper to line an 8 x 8 inch pan. This makes it easier to remove your magic bars.

2. In a large bowl, mix together the almond flour, Earth Balance, 1 tablespoon of maple syrup, and salt until it's well combined. Press into the pan in a thin layer. The dough will be crumbly and dry, but don't worry. It will hold together!

3. Sprinkle the shredded coconut, almond and chocolate over the base. Whisk together the coconut milk and 4 tablespoons of maple syrup, and pour it evenly over the toppings.

4. Bake for 40 minutes. It might look like it's getting over baked, but the maple syrup needs to caramelize, which is what darkens the color and gives a sweet, crisp crunch. Allow to cool, then chill in the fridge before cutting.

Store in an airtight container in the fridge or freeze for later use.

INGREDIENTS:

- 133 grams blanched almond flour (1¼ lightly filled cups)
- 1 tablespoon butter or softened coconut oil
- 1 tablespoon maple syrup
- ⅛ teaspoon salt
- 2 tablespoons shredded unsweetened coconut
- ⅔ cup slivered almonds or chopped pecans
- ⅔ cup chocolate chips or chopped chocolate bar
- 3 tablespoons full-fat canned coconut milk at room temperature
- 4 tablespoons maple syrup

Ice Box Peanut Butter Swirl Brownies

Grain and egg free, these moderately sweet, rich brownies stay chilled in the freezer. However, they will have a hard time staying in there for long. While they taste wonderful out of the oven, nothing compares to the fudgy texture that results after some time in the freezer. Coconut palm sugar or Sucanat perform the very best in this recipe.

Yield: One dozen brownies

DIRECTIONS:

1. Preheat oven to 350 degrees F. Oil a 7 x 7 inch square pan.

2. In the bowl of a stand mixer, combine all ingredients except for peanut butter. Mix until batter comes together. It will be very thick, more like a dough.

3. Place batter into pan. Coat a spatula in oil and use it to evenly press the dough into the pan.

4. Heat peanut butter in your microwave until melted. If your peanut butter remains thick, add some oil to thin it so that it is smooth. Drizzle the melted peanut butter onto the surface of the prepared brownies.

5. Place pan in oven and bake for 35 minutes. Remove from oven. Allow to cool completely before slicing. Place sliced brownies in a sealed bag or container and store in the freezer. Serve frozen.

INGREDIENTS:

- 140 grams blanched almond flour (1⅓ lightly filled cups)
- 172 grams potato starch (1 cup)
- 40 grams unsweetened cocoa powder (½ lightly filled cup)
- 1¼ cups coconut palm sugar or Sucanat
- ½ teaspoon baking powder
- ¼ teaspoon salt
- 1¼ teaspoons xanthan gum
- 60 grams unsweetened applesauce (½ cup)
- 131 grams mild flavored oil or melted butter (⅔ cup)
- 1 teaspoon vanilla extract
- ¼ cup melted peanut butter (or any other nut or seed butter)

Coconut & Lime Pound Cake

••

Zesty and bright, the flavor and texture of this pound cake will have you at first bite. Almond flour, the star in this recipe, packs a powerful nutritional punch and allows you to use less butter! Xylitol, a low glycemic sugar alternative, performs the best in this recipe. Although the other unrefined granulated sugars will work, they will create an extra moist cake.

Yield: One 9-inch loaf

Directions:

1. Preheat oven to 350 degrees F. Grease a 9-inch loaf pan.

2. In the bowl of a stand Mixer, beat butter, milk, xylitol, eggs and vanilla extract.

3. Add blanched almond flour, unsweetened coconut flakes, baking powder, salt, lime juice, and lime zest. Beat until thoroughly mixed.

4. Quickly pour batter into greased loaf pan and place in oven. Bake for 55-60 minutes until a toothpick inserted in the middle comes out clean.

5. While the loaf is baking, combine all custard ingredients in a saucepan over medium low heat. Whisk continually until custard becomes semi-thick. Remove from heat. Cover with plastic wrap and chill in fridge until ready to drizzle over the pound cake.

6. (Optional) Top the cake with toasted coconut flakes and additional lime zest.

Note: The coconut flakes play a role in soaking up some up the moisture in this pound cake. Using a brand that is finely ground Yields the best results.

Can be stored in an airtight container in the fridge, or frozen for later use.

Ingredients:

Cake:

4 tablespoons softened butter or melted coconut oil

½ cup milk

¾ cup xylitol

4 large eggs

1 teaspoon pure vanilla extract

247 grams blanched almond flour (2¼ packed cups)

41 grams fine unsweetened coconut flakes (⅔ cup)*

1 teaspoon baking powder

½ teaspoon salt

1 tablespoon freshly squeezed lime juice

Zest of one lime

Lime Custard Glaze:

½ cup full-fat canned coconut milk

2 large eggs

3 tablespoons freshly squeezed lime juice

Pinch of salt.

Sugar to taste (any sugar, refined or unrefined will work, including stevia)

Ask the Expert

. . . .

Our friend Elana Amsterdam is the author of *Gluten-Free Cupcakes* and *The Gluten-Free Almond Flour Cookbook*. Her blog, www.elanaspantry.com, is the go-to source for healthy, simple and always delicious recipes that often feature almond flour. We hope you enjoy her baking tips.

What should every new gluten-free baker know? Every baker, gluten-free or not, needs to start out with fresh, high-quality ingredients.

Do you have any money saving tips for gluten-free bakers? Use nutrient dense, filling ingredients so that you do not need to eat a ton to feel full and satiated. That's what I love about almond flour and coconut flour, so little goes such a long way.

What tips would you give for someone wanting to convert a family favorite recipe to gluten-free? Experiment. A lot.

What are your favorite flours to work with? Almond flour because it's a stand-alone flour that can be used without combining with numerous other flours and ingredients. Coconut flour, because it is light and fluffy, and makes great cakes and muffins. Flax meal because it imparts a rich nutty flavor to baked goods, and is especially delicious in breads.

How is almond flour different from other flours? I like almond flour so much that I wrote an entire book using it in each of 100 recipes. Almond flour has a very smooth texture, unlike some other gluten-free flours. It is also very special in that almonds are a superfood: high in protein, low in carbohydrates and full of amazing vitamins and minerals.

What type of recipes do you like to use Almond Flour in? I use it for all kinds of baked goods: cakes, cookies, breads, as well as for breading in dishes such as Eggplant Parmesan.

What kind of flours do you like to combine almond flour with? None, that's my favorite thing about it; it's easy!

How do you handle egg-free baking with almond flour? Given that I bake gluten-free, (mostly) dairy-free, and refined sugar free, I find that I need to use eggs for structure in my baking. Take away eggs, and I'm basically left with air since I don't use regular flour, butter or sugar. I do have one egg free recipe in my book *Gluten-Free Cupcakes* and I tested it 50 times until I was satisfied with that recipe.

What are your favorite types of recipes to bake and why? Cookies, power bars and bread are quick, easy, fun and tasty; and with almond flour, they're very healthy to boot.

What kind of gluten-free recipes would you suggest for a beginner to start with? Cookies, power bars and breads, when made with almond flour, are the simplest of gluten-free recipes with very few ingredients.

Do you bake by weight or volume? I bake by volume. I like to feel the measurements of the ingredients in my hands (I still use measuring cups!) even though this method is probably inferior. I love to use my kinesthetic senses in baking, which is why it is such an enjoyable outlet. For me, baking is meditative.

What kind of dairy free replacements do you like to bake with? Do you think the changes affect the texture and flavor? Coconut milk. Yes, sometimes using coconut imparts a coconut type taste. Sometimes not.

Can you give our readers some gluten-free bread making tips? Are there certain flours or other ingredients that you always use when making bread? I always use almond flour for breads. My favorite bread recipe right now is the high protein Paleo Bread on my website.

Chapter 3

Quinoa Flour

· ·

Quinoa is a magnificent flour. This is not something you likely expected to hear considering quinoa's bad flavor reputation. Back in 2010, Brittany was interested in the idea of creating homemade flours using sprouted grains and seeds. Her experimentation led her to discover that the soaking process lifted some of the bitter, grassy flavor from the quinoa. When it came time to dehydrate the seeds to make the flour, the flavor drastically improved. By the time the seeds made it to the flour grinding process, they had completely changed flavor and become mild and slightly sweet with a tinge of sourness. Intrigued by her discovery, Brittany did some baking experimentation with her homemade flour and was astounded with the great tasting results.

One year later, Brittany had the pleasure of meeting food scientist Linsey Herman. They discussed quinoa flour during their very first conversation and to their surprise, they had both discovered this unique change in quinoa. However, Linsey had found an easy shortcut: the grain did not need to be soaked and sprouted, it just simply needed toasting. We are pleased to now share this technique with you. Your baking experience with quinoa is about to drastically change. Here's how:

Preparing quinoa flour is an easy process. Here is Linsey's simple process:

1. Preheat your oven to 215 degrees F.

2. Cover two rimmed cookie sheets each with a piece of parchment paper or aluminum foil

3. Pour 1 bag (1 pound) of quinoa flour onto the two covered cookie sheets. Spread it out so that it is no more than ¼-½ inch deep.

4. Place in the oven and set timer for 2½ hours. During this time you will notice the quinoa's strong smell diminish a little at a time until the aroma is gone.

5. After the 2½ hours, remove from the oven and store in a container. Due to its fat content, we suggest you store it in the fridge or freezer as quinoa has the tendency to go rancid quickly.

Note: All recipes in this chapter call for prepared quinoa flour. Neglecting to prepare the flour will result in baked goods that have a strong, unpleasant flavor. If you've worked with quinoa flour before and like the taste, feel free to use it without preparing it first.

Nutritional Highlights:

This ancient seed is a complete protein containing all nine essential amino acids and a host of beneficial phytonutrients and minerals including manganese, a mineral with a powerful antioxidant capacity.

Brand Comparison:

Most brands of quinoa flour are comparable. The standout brand we recommend is Dakota Prairie. It stands above the rest for its mild, less grassy flavor, and it is finely ground. We still found that it needed to be heat treated, but for a shorter period of time.

- **Dakota Prairie**

Best Flours to Substitute for Quinoa Flour:

Sorghum and Garbanzo Bean flour: Sorghum and garbanzo will provide a different texture, but due to their similar high protein count we found they could be replaced in a 1:1 ratio with fairly good results.

Brown Rice Flour: This can be used in a 1:1 ratio with quinoa flour. It has a lower protein content so recipes may not rise as well and will result in a denser product.

Teff and Millet Flour: We recommend these flours as a last resort. As they are not heavy they will rise similarly to quinoa, but they will give your baked goods a vastly different taste and texture. You can sub them in a 1:1 ratio.

Quinoa Flour Tips:

- Has a slight sour aftertaste that works great for recipes like English muffins or sourdough. This "sour" flavor is mild enough that it also will work well is sweet applications when balanced with strong flavors.

- Works as a bread flour due to its high protein levels which help provide structure, shape and rise.

- Works well in pastry applications.

- Has a bitter flavor that can be mitigated by treating the flour as described above. Some people like the flavor and prefer to bake without treating it. Try it both ways to decide which you prefer.

- If not heat treated, the flour should only be used in applications in which it is combined with strong flavors. Chocolate, coffee and hazelnut are all good examples.

- Can create light baked goods when combined with eggs and starch.

- Quinoa is a middle of the road flour; it is soft, but not overly so. This makes it great as an all-purpose flour.

Fun uses for quinoa

- Quinoa flakes are a delicious alternative to rolled oats for hot cereal, cookies, and any recipes calling for oats.

- Quinoa in its grain form is a great gluten-free alternative to rice, and can be used in many cooking applications.

English Muffins

. . . .

*Cooked on the stove top, these English muffins
are filled with nooks and crannies galore. Complete with a slightly sour taste, they will take
you back to your gluten eating days. Use your
kitchen scale for the very best results.*

Yield: Four muffins

DIRECTIONS:

1. Combine the lukewarm water with the yeast and sugar. Mix and set aside for 5 minutes. If yeast does not begin to bubble, start over with fresh yeast, sugar and water.

2. Combine the quinoa flour, rice flour, potato starch, xanthan gum, salt, and baking powder. Mix well.

3. Stir in the bubbling yeast mixture and the oil. Mix until fully incorporated. The dough will be fairly wet.

4. Place four English muffin rings in a large skillet. Oil each ring. Sprinkle the pan with a little cornmeal (optional).

5. Place equal amounts of the dough into each ring. Drizzle a little oil on top of each mound of dough to prevent sticking and then use a spoon to gently press the dough down into a circular disk shape in the rings. Sprinkle with a little more cornmeal (optional).

6. Cover the skillet with a lid. Turn the stove top on under the skillet on low for 1 minute. Turn off heat, keeping English muffins covered and allow them to rise for 15-18 minutes.

7. After the 15-18 minutes, turn the burner back on to medium-low heat. Keep lid on and cook the English muffins for 10 minutes. Remove lid and flip the English muffins so the other side can cook. Remove the English muffins rings.

8. Re-cover the skillet and cook for another 10 minutes.

9. Remove the finished English muffins from skillet and break open using a fork.

Note: English muffin rings can be purchased at most specialty cooking stores. You can also make your own by folding aluminum foil over itself and creating rings. Use metal paperclips to hold them together.

To serve: Place the English muffins in toaster and then butter liberally! Store extra English muffins at room temperature in a sealed container or freeze for another day.

INGREDIENTS:

176 grams lukewarm water (¾ cup + 1 tablespoon)

11 grams fast acting yeast (1 tablespoon)

1½ teaspoons granulated sugar (any variety)

70 grams prepared quinoa flour (½ packed cup)

30 grams superfine rice flour (¼ packed cup)

106 grams potato starch (¾ cup)

¼ teaspoon xanthan gum

½ teaspoon salt

1½ teaspoon double acting baking powder

1 teaspoon oil

Cornmeal for dusting (optional)

Garlic & Rosemary Focaccia

Afraid to make gluten-free bread for the first time? This recipe is for you. It's easy to make, hard to screw up and fabulous with any meal. It's no wonder focaccia is a favorite among so many. For variation, put your creativity to work and add different spice combinations to the dough and topping of this bread. We especially loved it with caramelized onions, sea salt and rosemary on top.

Yield: One 9-inch round focaccia

DIRECTIONS:

1. Preheat oven to 375 degrees F. Oil a pie pan or 9 inch round cake pan.

2. Combine the lukewarm water, yeast, and honey. Mix well and set aside for 5 minutes allowing mixture to froth and bubble.

3. In a bowl, combine the quinoa flour, rice flour, potato starch, xanthan gum, garlic powder, rosemary, pepper, and salt. Mix well.

4. Stir the yeast/water mixture into the flour mixture. Add the egg and oil. Mix for 1-2 minutes.

5. Place mixture into oiled pan. Drizzle with a little oil and top with some coarsely ground sea salt, pepper, and rosemary. *Note:* to get the little holes in the surface that you see pictured, poke an oiled finger evenly across the dough to leave indentation marks.

6. Cover with a towel and place in a warm location to rise for 15-18 minutes.

7. Once dough has risen, place into oven and bake for 30 minutes.

8. Remove from oven and allow to cool 15-20 minutes before eating.

Note: All of our bread recipes will have better results using grams versus cups. Yeast breads are finicky and you want to make sure you're measuring the flours correctly. For this recipe we use the microwave proofing box technique (see section on how to make yeast breads).

If not eating immediately, let it cool to room temperature and store in a sealed container on your counter top or freeze for later use.

INGREDIENTS:

290 grams lukewarm water (1¼ cup)

2¼ teaspoons fast acting yeast

1 tablespoon agave or honey (or other liquid sweetener)

124 grams prepared quinoa flour (1 packed cup)

63 grams superfine rice flour (brown or white) (½ packed cup)

166 grams potato starch (1 cup)

¾ teaspoon xanthan gum

1 tablespoon garlic powder

2 teaspoons dried rosemary

½ teaspoon pepper

1 teaspoon salt

1 large egg

1 tablespoon oil

Sesame & Garlic Crackers

Rustic, thin and crispy these crackers are perfect for any occasion. The garlic and sesame flavor is addictive and we're sure you'll want to make these time and time again.

Yield: Three cookie sheets

DIRECTIONS:

1. Preheat oven to 350 degrees F.

2. In a large bowl, combine the quinoa flour, rice flour, potato starch, xanthan gum, baking powder, garlic powder, salt, and sesame seeds.

3. Add the water and oil. Using your hands, knead the dough until it comes together. Divide dough into 3 balls.

4. Roll each ball between two sheets of parchment paper using a heavy rolling pin. Roll out as thin as possible. Remove the top layer of parchment and cut the dough using a pizza cutter or sharp knife into squares (or triangles!) Do not separate the pieces.

5. Transport this sheet of parchment to the cookie sheet and bake 25-28 minutes.

6. Remove from oven and allow to cool.

Note: It is best to roll out all 3 mounds of dough right away, and to bake 2 trays at once. As the dough sits, the baking powder will begin to work and the longer they sit uncooked the less they will puff up in the oven.

Store crackers at room temp in a sealed bag or container.

INGREDIENTS:

62 grams prepared quinoa flour (½ packed cup)

63 grams superfine rice flour (brown or white) (½ packed cup)

125 grams potato starch (¾ cup)

1 teaspoon xanthan gum

1 tablespoon + 1 teaspoon double acting baking powder

1 tablespoon garlic powder

1 teaspoon salt

½ cup sesame seeds

½ cup + 2 tablespoons water

6 tablespoons oil (olive oil or sesame oil are especially great!)

Hazelnut Espresso Shortbread Cookies

Quick to make, these cookies are a sophisticated treat. For a little variation, substitute the hazelnut meal for any other nut or seed meal.

Yield: Two dozen cookies

DIRECTIONS:

1. Preheat oven to 350 degrees F.

2. If the sugar you have selected has large granules, run it through a coffee grinder, this will make for a cookie with a cohesive texture.

3. In a food processor, combine all ingredients until they come together into a crumbly dough.

4. Roll dough out on a non-stick surface until it is ¼ inch thick. If you find the dough is too crumbly to roll, you may add up to 1 tablespoon of water. After rolling, cut out using cookie cutter.

5. Place on cookie sheet and bake 15-18 minutes.

6. Drizzle cooled cookies with melted chocolate.

Note: To melt chocolate, select your favorite chocolate chips or bar and place in a microwave safe bowl. Heat 1-2 minutes, stopping the microwave to stir every 30 seconds until fully melted.

INGREDIENTS:

75 grams quinoa flour (½ packed cup)

60 grams hazelnut meal (½ packed cup)

50 grams tapioca starch (½ cup)

2 tablespoons coffee or espresso grounds

6 tablespoons powdered unrefined granulated sugar

90 grams butter (6 tablespoons)

1 tablespoon pure vanilla extract

Melted chocolate to drizzle on top

Buttermilk Biscuits

Soft and tender, these delicious biscuits will melt in your mouth. When made with bacon lard, that flavor enters a level of indescribable bliss. As with most rice-based recipes, these taste best when warm.

Yield: 8-10 biscuits

DIRECTIONS:

1. Preheat oven to 450 degrees F.

2. Combine the milk and vinegar in a small cup to create "buttermilk" and set aside.

3. In a large bowl, combine the rice flour, quinoa flour, tapioca starch, xanthan gum, salt, baking powder and baking soda.

4. Cut the butter into the flour mixture until it is pea sized.

5. Gently stir in the buttermilk. Do not over mix. The dough will feel semi-wet.

6. Heavily flour a surface with additional tapioca starch then place dough on floured surface and liberally cover it with starch. Cover your hands with tapioca to prevent the dough from sticking to your hands.

7. Gently pat dough so that it is ½-1 inch thick. Using a biscuit cutter or a round glass, cut the dough and place on cookie sheet.

8. Quickly place into the oven and bake 12-15 minutes. Serve warm.

Note: Making biscuits is a bit of an art form. It is important that the dough is not over mixed; doing so will change the texture. When making these biscuits, stir just until the flours have come together to form a dough.

INGREDIENTS:

223 grams milk (1⅛ cup)

1½ tablespoons vinegar or lemon juice

98 grams superfine rice flour (brown or white) (¾ packed cup)

65 grams prepared quinoa flour (½ packed cup)

123 grams tapioca starch (1 cup)

1 teaspoon xanthan gum

1 teaspoon salt

½ teaspoon double acting baking powder

1½ teaspoons baking soda

6 tablespoons butter or bacon lard

Maple-Pecan Muffins

Hearty and moist, these muffins will make any morning wonderful. Maple syrup and pecans complement quinoa's flavor.

Yield: 18 muffins

DIRECTIONS:

1. Preheat oven to 325 degrees F. Prepare 18 muffin cups by greasing them or putting in muffin liners.

2. In a small bowl, combine the milk and vinegar to create a buttermilk. Set aside.

3. In a large bowl, combine quinoa flour, rice flour, tapioca starch, xanthan gum, sugar, baking powder, baking soda, cinnamon, and salt.

4. Stir in the "buttermilk," vanilla extract, maple syrup and melted butter. Stir in the chopped pecans.

5. Quickly scoop the batter into the muffin cups, filling almost to the brim.

6. Drizzle an additional ¼ cup of maple syrup over the top of the batter.

7. Bake 20-23 minutes, until a toothpick inserted in the middle comes out clean.

Store in an airtight container once cooled and store at room temperature or freeze for another day.

INGREDIENTS:

345 grams milk (1½ cups)

7 grams vinegar (2 teaspoons)

127 grams prepared quinoa flour (1 packed cup)

124 grams superfine brown or white rice flour (1 packed cup)

86 grams tapioca starch (⅔ cup)

1 teaspoon xanthan gum

½ cup unrefined granulated sugar

1½ teaspoons baking powder

½ teaspoon baking soda

2½ teaspoons cinnamon

½ teaspoon salt

1 teaspoon pure vanilla extract

¾ cup maple syrup

6½ tablespoons melted butter or oil

1 cup chopped pecans

¼ cup maple syrup

Red Velvet Doughnut Holes

These cake-like doughnut holes are fun to make and taste best the day they are made. You will never guess from their taste that they were made of mostly whole grain flours. Our recipe testers loved these little morsels.

Yield: 2-3 dozen doughnut holes

DIRECTIONS:

1. Pour several cups of oil into a heavy bottomed sauce pan. Turn the burner on medium heat and begin heating the oil. The ideal temperature is between 305-325 degrees F. Test this using a candy thermometer.

2. In the bowl of a stand mixer, combine the dry ingredients: rice flour, quinoa flour, tapioca starch, xanthan gum, sugar, cocoa powder, baking soda, baking powder, and salt.

3. Add the wet ingredients: egg, oil, vanilla extract, buttermilk, and food coloring. Mix until the dough comes together. It will be extremely sticky.

4. Heavily flour a clean surface with tapioca starch. Using a spatula, place the mound of sticky dough on the pile of tapioca starch. Cover all sides of the dough with the tapioca so that it is no longer sticky.

5. Using your hands, press the dough out so that it is 1 inch thick. Using a small circular floured biscuit cutter, cut as many doughnut holes as you can out of this sheet. It will be hard to go back and re-use the dough after this round so squeeze them in tight. If, at any point, the dough becomes sticky, add more tapioca.

6. Once the oil has reached the designated heat, test one or two doughnut holes. If the heat is too low the doughnuts will not puff up properly. If the heat is too high it will burn the doughnuts. Adjust heat to find the happy medium.

7. Fry the doughnut holes 3-4 minutes, being sure to flip them several times during the frying process.

Carefully remove them from the oil and place them on a clean paper towel to drain. Allow to cool.

Tip: Working with cold ingredients makes for less sticky dough. We store flours in the freezer and pull them out just before measuring and mixing this dough. You must use cane sugar in this recipe. Unrefined sugars contribute different amounts of moisture to baked goods so changing the sugar could fatally affect the end result of these doughnuts.

INGREDIENTS:

Oil for frying: We like to use the healthier oils and suggest refined coconut oil or grapeseed oil.

100 grams superfine white or brown rice flour (½ packed cup)

80 grams prepared quinoa flour (¾ packed cup)

100 grams tapioca starch (¾ cup)

1 teaspoon xanthan gum

1⅛ cup organic cane sugar (granulated)

2 tablespoons unsweetened cocoa powder

1 tablespoon double acting baking powder

1 teaspoon baking soda

¼ teaspoon salt

1 large egg

2 tablespoons mild flavored oil

1 teaspoon pure vanilla extract

½ cup milk + 1⅛ teaspoons vinegar to make a buttermilk

½-1 bottle red food coloring (optional)

INGREDIENTS:

113 grams (prepared) quinoa flour (¾ packed cup)

62 grams superfine brown rice flour (½ packed cup)

86 grams potato starch (½ cup)

80 grams unsweetened cocoa powder (1 lightly filled cup)

1 teaspoon xanthan gum

2 cups unrefined granulated sugar

2 teaspoons double acting baking powder

¼ teaspoon salt

2 Eggs

1¼ cup full-fat canned coconut milk

1 tablespoon apple cider vinegar (or other vinegar)

1 teaspoon pure vanilla extract

⅔ cup mild flavored oil

Devil's Food Cake

A healthier take on Devil's Food Cake comprised mostly of whole grains! This recipe is proof that prepared quinoa flour works well in sweet applications.

Yield: One 9-inch cake

DIRECTIONS:

1. Preheat oven to 350 degrees F. Oil a 9 inch cake pan.

2. In a bowl, combine quinoa flour, brown rice flour, potato starch, cocoa powder, xanthan gum, sugar, baking powder, and salt.

3. Add the eggs, coconut milk, apple cider vinegar, vanilla extract and oil. Using a hand mixer (or stand mixer), beat the batter until fully mixed.

4. Pour into prepared cake pan and bake 45-50 minutes (until toothpick inserted in the middle comes out clean.) Allow cake to cool completely before slicing.

Note: This basic Devil's Food Cake can be frosted with your favorite frosting recipe. Try drizzling a chocolate glaze on top or see our frosting section for Buttercream Frosting!

Ask the Expert

. . . .

Meet Linsey Herman, the Harvard- and Northwestern-educated pastry chef. She is a former chef and head of Research & Development at Enjoy Life Foods, where she developed many of its products. Linsey is a food science genius and was an integral piece in the development of these books. We are so excited that she agreed to share many of her gluten-free tips with us. Read closely and enjoy!

How long have you been baking gluten-free? I've been baking since 2005, when my nutritionist suggested that I had gluten intolerance. I had a lot of chronic conditions—some which required medication—and others that required maintenance. When I stopped eating gluten, I was able to go cold turkey off one of my medications and the symptoms of other conditions lessened. It was amazing. I started playing with gluten-free grains almost immediately. Although I'm trained as a pastry chef, I've never been a big consumer of baked goods, I guess because I've probably eaten my fill in the kitchens where I've worked. So making the transition away from gluten was relatively easy.

Do you ever use commercial gluten-free all-purpose mixes? Never ever ever! Making your own mix is one of the easiest things you can do. Making a cup-for-cup equivalent mix isn't rocket science and just requires common sense and a desire to experiment. My all-purpose mix has a combination of flours, mostly whole grain with just enough starch to lighten it up.

What flours do you like to use to make cake? I am very sensitive to flavors on the bitter spectrum, so I tend to avoid any flours that leave strong aftertastes. I've used all kinds of flours depending on the type of cake I'm making. I've found that an all-purpose mix of 75 percent sorghum and 25 percent tapioca starch is simple and works well.

What flours do you like to use when making cookies? Nut flours, coconut flour, sorghum and a little starch, if necessary.

What flours besides rice do you find work well exchanged for each other? Sorghum is a great, all-purpose flour and underutilized by home bakers. It can be swapped in for so many flours (like buckwheat or teff or millet) and doesn't have a strong aftertaste. It should be balanced with a little starch—rice, potato, tapioca or arrowroot.

What are the top three things every new gluten-free baker should know?

1. Store your whole grain flours and nut flours in the freezer. There's nothing worse than a baked good made with rancid flour.

2. Make your own mixes, and don't be afraid to experiment. A failed baked good isn't a tragedy; it is a learning experience.

3. Buy the finest flour you can afford, in terms of quality and grain size, and make your own if you can. The more fine the grain (especially with rice flour), the less sandy the product will taste. If you buy in bulk, you'll save money—but make sure you have a place in your freezer that will hold your flour. And keep it in an airtight container so it doesn't take on the odor of the freezer.

Do you have any money saving tips for gluten-free bakers? Make your own almond flour if you can—the stuff you buy in stores is crazy expensive and can be rancid if your market doesn't move a lot of it. Gums aren't necessary in all baked goods and in some cases just make things gummy and wet. If you have eggs in a recipe, you probably won't need much gum, if any.

What tips would you give for someone wanting to convert a family favorite recipe to gluten-free? Make sure the grain you buy is as finely milled as the flour you are used to using in your family recipes! And don't be disappointed if it takes a few tries to get it right.

Can you tell us a bit about quinoa flour? What kind of recipes do you find it works best? Quinoa flour is very tricky—it tastes like soap and grass if it is used in most recipes without some treatment. I didn't realize this the first time I baked with it. The cake I made was perfect and looked exactly like the cakes I made with wheat flour—but it was inedible. I did some reading and learned that the saponins on the outside of the quinoa seed—a natural defense against predators—are mostly to blame for this and even though some companies market their quinoa flour as double and triple washed, quinoa still tastes off. Wet heat and dry heat are needed to minimize the unpleasant flavor. If you make a dumpling dough with quinoa and steam or boil it, you'd reduce those off-flavors. And if you gently toast the dry flour in a kiln or oven or fry pan (if you don't have an oven) you can also make it taste better. If you compare the aroma of the toasted quinoa to the untoasted quinoa, you'll see how much of the unpleasant aromatics are heated off in the process.

What's the most challenging recipe you ever developed and why? My friend Sara Boswell, who is a sorghum scientist, and I decided to make egg-free, dairy-free, gluten-free, nut-free donuts and it took us more than a day of iterations to get the recipe right with both of us weighing in on changes. It was complicated because there were so many variables—fat, sugar, egg substitute, leavening acid—and all of it was interrelated. If we changed the order in which we added ingredients, we'd get an unpleasant aftertaste or color. At the end of the day—I think we did about 12 batches—we finally found the ratio and order to make light, fluffy, delicious donuts. Unfortunately they staled within about 24 hours, a common problem in gluten-free baking.

What kind of dairy free replacements do you like to bake with? Do you think the changes affect the texture and flavor? I use a lot of water to replace fluid milk and sustainable palm oil, coconut oil, and sometimes even vegan buttery spreads in place of butter. Butter is magical in baked goods and there's simply no true substitute for it, though toasted nut flour in a recipe could give a little more of that 'noisette' quality in something made without it. Palm oil is nearly 100% fat, versus butter which is typically 80-82% fat. When using something like palm, there really can't be a 1:1 exchange for butter—it should be closer to 3:4 exchange.

What differences have you noticed between tapioca starch, potato starch, and arrowroot starch? How do you decide which you want to use in a recipe? I really try to avoid using starches in my recipes and almost never use potato starch. Arrowroot is too expensive—and too gummy for my taste. I generally like to use tapioca because it isn't wildly expensive and a little goes a long way.

Can you give our readers some gluten-free bread making tips? Are there certain flours or other ingredients that you always use when making bread? Protein, protein, protein—gluten-free bread needs protein! Not too much, but enough to help the sides of the bread form a strong structure as it bakes, or it will collapse on itself. Egg whites are the tried and true protein source, but bean flours and whey powder will work well too. If you combine all of them, you can get a really sturdy sandwich loaf. If you can't use eggs, whey, or bean flours, make rounded buns, mini loaves, flatbread or grissini or baguettes instead of loaves. They won't collapse on you. I've used rice protein and quinoa protein in breads and it definitely works—just not as well as eggs.

Chapter 4

Amaranth Flour

· ·

When we developed the idea for this cookbook, we wanted recipes that would feature each flour prominently. In our almond flour chapter, we have recipes that only use almond flour. In our buckwheat flour chapter, we have recipes using only buckwheat and starch. With amaranth flour, that was almost impossible to do. You'll notice two things about this chapter. First, we only have four recipes. Second, only one recipe features amaranth exclusively; the rest use amaranth, starch and brown or white rice flour. Here's why: Amaranth flour has a very distinct smell and flavor that can be overpowering. One friend told us the bag of amaranth flour smelled like cement. Now to be fair, when cooked, it adds a nutty flavor to recipes that some people will like and some won't.

Before you move onto another chapter, let's talk about why you might want to stock amaranth in your pantry. We developed these recipes to work with the flavor of amaranth, and we absolutely loved how they turned out. Amaranth flour is finely ground and it creates a soft texture that we haven't noticed with the other flours. By adding a small amount of amaranth to your recipes (enough to help the texture but not so much that you'll taste it), you can achieve a softer result. In general, a bag of amaranth will last a long time because only a very little will be used in the recipes (unless you fall in love with our mocha biscotti). So go out and grab a bag and throw it in the freezer to have on hand.

Nutritional Highlights:

Not only is amaranth a complete protein, containing all nine essential amino acids, it has also been shown to have cancer-preventative, anti-inflammatory, and anti-hypertensive effects.

Brand Comparison:

We haven't noticed a difference in brands of amaranth flour. The brands we've worked with have been equally successful:

- **Dakota Prairie**
- **Nuts.com**
- **Bob's Red Mill**

Best flours to substitute for amaranth flour:

Garbanzo, sorghum, millet, teff, quinoa, buckwheat, brown rice, and white rice flour: Amaranth flour is very soft, and because of this, it doesn't give recipes the same structure that some other flours do. If you substitute these flours for amaranth in our recipes you will achieve similar results, but you may notice some will rise better. For instance, if you take the amaranth out of the brownies and substitute teff flour, the result will be less fudgy and more cake-like. You can substitute the flours in a 1:1 ratio.

Amaranth Flour Tips:

- To get around the strong smell, we recommend using it in recipes that contain other strong flavors (like chocolate and coffee). Only use as much as you need to achieve the desired texture. The rest of the recipe can be made using a flour with a flavor you prefer.

- In bread, a very small amount of amaranth flour can be used to create a softer texture (start with ¼ cup).

We don't recommend using amaranth in our vegan pancakes. They will be flat and uncooked inside.

Fun uses for amaranth

- The seeds can be popped into miniature amaranth popcorn, just as you would with corn kernels!

- Use amaranth seeds to make a high-fiber, hot breakfast cereal. Drizzle with maple syrup and enjoy!

Sweet Cornbread

We love to pair the mild sweetness of this cornbread with a spicy chili. Enjoy it for a casual dinner or a summer picnic.

Yield: 16 squares

DIRECTIONS:

1. Lightly oil an 8 x 8 inch baking dish. Preheat the oven to 425 degrees F.

2. In a medium-sized bowl, whisk together the cornmeal, amaranth flour, brown rice flour, potato starch, baking powder, and salt.

3. In a small bowl, stir together the flax, psyllium, and water. Set aside.

4. In a large bowl, beat the eggs and sugar on high speed for 2 minutes. Turn speed down to medium and add in the flax/psyllium mix, oil, milk, and dry ingredients until mixed in. Once they're mixed, turn the speed back up to high and beat for 3 minutes. Turn beater off and fold in the corn.

5. Pour into the baking dish. Sprinkle with ¾ teaspoon sugar (and ¼ teaspoon cinnamon if using). Bake for 35 minutes or until a toothpick inserted in the middle comes out clean. Serve warm.

Store in an airtight container in the fridge or freeze for later use.

INGREDIENTS:

205 grams cornmeal (1¼ cups)

27 grams amaranth flour (¼ lightly filled cup)

32 grams brown rice flour (¼ lightly filled cup)

43 grams potato starch (¼ cup)

3 teaspoons double acting baking powder

¾ teaspoon salt

1 tablespoon ground flax seed meal

1 tablespoon whole psyllium husks

6 tablespoons boiling water

3 large eggs

½ cup unrefined granulated sugar

1 tablespoon mild flavored oil

½ cup unsweetened milk

1 cup canned or frozen corn (thawed if frozen)

¾ teaspoon unrefined granulated sugar

¼ teaspoon ground cinnamon (optional)

Cilantro Pesto Stuffed Skillet Rolls

These tasty dinner rolls are quite the lookers and are conveniently made in a skillet. The nutty flavor of the amaranth compliments the fresh pesto. We encourage creative minds to run wild with this recipe; just about any pesto recipe can be used as the filling.

Yield: One dozen rolls

Directions:

To make this recipe you will need a heavy bottomed skillet with a lid! I use a cast iron skillet and a clear glass lid that fits on top. These can also be baked in the oven at 375 degrees F for 17-20 minutes once the dough has risen. The stovetop method is more fun and creates a delicious crust on the bottom of the rolls.

1. Make the pesto by combining all the ingredients in a food processor. Set aside.

2. Turn oven on to 350 degrees F. Once it reaches this temperature, turn it off and keep the oven door shut.

3. Prepare a 9-inch skillet by drizzling 1 tablespoon of oil and spreading it out on the pan surface.

4. In a small bowl, combine the lukewarm water, yeast and sugar. Set aside to proof.

5. In the bowl of a stand mixer, make the dough: Combine the rice flour, amaranth flour, tapioca starch, potato flour, xanthan gum, baking powder, sugar, and salt. Pour in the water/yeast mixture,, eggs, and oil. Mix on high until the dough becomes very sticky (and begins to stick to the bowl).

6. Oil a large sheet of parchment paper. Using a spatula, plop the sticky glob of dough onto the center of the prepared parchment. Drizzle a little additional oil on the surface of your dough and hands. Using your hands press the dough into an 18 x 10 inch rectangular shape. Cover the surface with the prepared pesto.

Ingredients:

Pesto Filling:
- 1 bunch packed cilantro (2 cups)
- 1½ teaspoons ground cumin
- 2 tablespoons garlic powder
- ½ teaspoon salt
- ½ teaspoon black pepper
- 3-4 tablespoons olive oil
- 2 tablespoons roasted sesame seeds (optional)

Pan:
- 1 tablespoon oil

Rolls:
- 260 grams lukewarm water (1 cup + 2 tablespoons)
- 2 teaspoons sugar
- 1 tablespoon fast acting yeast
- 127 grams superfine white rice flour (1 packed cup)
- 64 grams amaranth flour (½ packed cup)
- 160 grams tapioca starch (1¼ cup)
- 32 grams potato starch (¼ cup)
- 2¼ teaspoons xanthan gum
- 1 tablespoon double acting baking powder
- ⅓ cup granulated sugar (any variety except coconut palm or xylitol)
- ½ teaspoon salt
- 2 large eggs

7. Using the parchment paper as your guide, roll the dough up (as you would cinnamon rolls). After rolling, dust the surface with a little rice flour for easier handling. Slice the dough into 12 rolls using a piece of dental floss for a clean cut.

8. Place the rolls side by side in the prepared skillet. Cover with a lid and place on a burner. Turn on high for 1-2 minutes to get the skillet warm. Turn off the heat, keeping the lid intact and let the rolls rise for 25 minutes.

9. After the 25 minutes, keep the lid on and turn the burner back on to medium-low heat. Cook for ten minutes. Meanwhile preheat the oven to 375 degrees F.

10. After the ten minutes of cooking time on the stove top, remove the lid, brush the rolls with a little oil and bake them in the oven for 12-14 minutes. After this cooking time if you would like your rolls to have some additional golden brown color, place them under the broiler briefly.

11. Serve warm right out of the skillet.

Note: Store rolls at room temperature in a sealed container or bag or freeze for another day. Reheat briefly prior to serving.

Whiskey Brownies

. . . .

These decadent brownies are delicious served warm from the oven with a scoop of vanilla ice cream. For those of you who don't like raisins, don't worry. You can't taste them at all! Have fun with these and try replacing the whiskey with rum or liqueur. If you prefer alcohol-free brownies, you can use milk instead.

Yield: 16 brownies

DIRECTIONS:

1. Preheat the oven to 350 degrees F. Lightly oil an 8 x 8 inch baking pan.

2. Put the chia seeds, raisins, whiskey, oil, and vanilla extract in a food processor and blend until the raisins are completely chopped.

3. Whisk together the sugar, brown rice flour, amaranth flour, cocoa powder, baking soda, and salt in a medium-sized bowl, then pour into the food processor and blend completely with the wet ingredients.

4. Scoop into the pan and smooth evenly. Bake for 40 minutes. These can be served warm, room temperature, or chilled in the fridge.

Store in an airtight container in the fridge or freeze for later use.

INGREDIENTS:

1 tablespoon ground chia seeds or whole psyllium husks

½ cup raisins

½ cup whiskey

¼ cup mild flavored oil

1 tablespoon pure vanilla extract

1 cup unrefined granulated sugar

65 grams brown rice flour (½ lightly filled cup)

136 grams amaranth flour (⅓ lightly filled cup)

26 grams unsweetened cocoa powder (⅓ lightly filled cup)

½ teaspoon baking soda

½ teaspoon salt

Mocha Biscotti

. . . .

These are not your typical biscotti. We wanted to create a recipe for the non-biscotti loving crowd, so we made these on the moist side. If you prefer your biscotti super crunchy, bake them for an extra 2-3 minutes.

Yield: One dozen biscotti

DIRECTIONS:

1. Preheat the oven to 350 degrees F. Place a piece of parchment paper on a cookie sheet.

2. In a medium-sized bowl, whisk the amaranth flour, cocoa, baking soda, baking powder, and salt. Set aside.

3. Pour hot coffee over psyllium husks and flax seeds in a mug. Stir briefly, then let sit while preparing the rest of the ingredients.

4. In a large bowl, cream the shortening, sugar and milk with a hand beater on low speed. Beat the coffee mixture in completely, then pour in the dry ingredients, continuing to beat on low until completely mixed.

5. Shape dough into a log on the parchment paper (on cookie sheet) and flatten to about an inch thick (it should be about 5 x 7 inches). It will be sticky, so you can wet your fingertips if needed to help smooth it out. Bake for 30 minutes.

6. Remove from oven. Turn oven down to 300 degrees F. Let dough cool for 15 minutes on the cookie sheet (if using a baking stone, remove parchment paper from stone so it will cool). Remove the parchment paper from cookie sheet and cut the log into 12 slices. It will be delicate at this point so be careful of crumbling, but will hold together well once completely baked. Place the slices back on the cookie sheet. Bake for another 20 minutes at 300 degrees F. Let cool completely.

Can be stored in an airtight container at room temperature.

INGREDIENTS:

109 grams amaranth flour (1 lightly filled cup)

20 grams unsweetened cocoa powder (¼ lightly filled cup)

¾ teaspoon baking soda

½ teaspoon baking powder

½ teaspoon salt

1½ teaspoons whole psyllium husks or ground chia seeds

1½ teaspoons ground flax seed meal

2 tablespoons hot coffee

¼ cup plus 2 tablespoons shortening

½ cup unrefined granulated sugar

3 tablespoons unsweetened milk

Ask the Expert

. . . .

Beth Hillson is the food editor of Living Without Magazine, the president of the American Celiac Disease Alliance, and the creator of the popular Gluten-Free Pantry products. Most recently she authored Gluten-Free Makeovers, a book of family favorites made gluten-free.

How long have you been baking gluten-free? I have been baking gluten free since I was diagnosed with celiac disease in 1976.

Do you remember the first thing you ever baked gluten-free? I found a cookbook written by Marion Woods. It was the only thing available at the time. I made her recipe for lemon drop cookies. I remember that the recipe called for soy flour, which was something I could purchase in a local store. I hadn't had any baked goods in months so these tasted delicious. Then I made pizza on corn tortillas. That was my idea.

Do you ever use commercial gluten-free all-purpose mixes? I use all-purpose mixes, especially when I'm short on time or when I am missing ingredients to make my own blends. I'm happy to take a shortcut as long as I am sure it won't diminish the outcome. My favorite is Gluten-Free Pantry All-Purpose Flour, of course. I created it! I also like Bob's Red Mill All-Purpose Flour. It has protein in it.

What flours do you like to use to make cake? Cake flour has a little cornstarch in it (2 tablespoons per cup of flour). So I add cornstarch to my flour blend when I make cakes and cupcakes. I also use sorghum flour, extra fine brown or white rice flour and a second starch, usually tapioca starch.

What flours do you like to use to make cookies? This is one time when I prefer the white flours—rice, sweet rice, cornstarch, potato starch, tapioca starch. Cookies should have a delicate crumb and some of the other flours impart a taste that can be overpowering. If I want a chewy cookie, however, I will add a small amount of potato flour or use gluten-free oats or oat flour.

What flours do you find work best in place of rice flour? Sorghum is the closest substitution, in my opinion. But corn flour and buckwheat flour are also good substitutes. None are quite as neutral in flavor as rice flour, and buckwheat imparts a distinctive flecked look to baked goods. However, all three can be used as 1:1 replacements for rice flour as baking characteristics are similar.

What are the top three things every new gluten-free baker should know?
1. **Substitute Boldly.** By that I mean, when you see a recipe that's filled with gluten-containing ingredients, imagine which gluten-free ingredients can be substituted to make it something you can have.

2. **Live With, Not Without.** Make a list of foods you cannot eat and pair each one with something you can have. As you get more adept at changing out ingredients, your list of ingredients you can have will grow longer and your confidence will grow as well.

3. **The success of gluten-free baking is basically finding the best ratio of liquid to dry ingredients in each recipe. It's like making rice.** Too much water and the rice is like mush; too little and it's brittle and crunchy.

Do you have any money saving tips for gluten-free bakers? The first time you try a new recipe, make half of the recipe to see if it works and if you like it. If it doesn't turn out, you've wasted fewer ingredients. If you love the recipe, you'll make it again and might even double it. If the recipe is for a bread or cake, scoop dough or batter into muffin cups and bake for a shorter amount of time (18 minutes for cupcakes; 22 to 25 for yeast breads). When you find a blend of flours you like, buy in bulk. Amazon sells cases of flours at reasonable prices. You'll find good prices at big box stores like Walmart, Ocean State Job Lot and Price Chopper, too. However, selection might be limited. Bob's Red Mill sells their own flours in 5 and 25 pound bags.

What tips would you give for someone wanting to convert a family favorite recipe to gluten-free? I wrote a whole book on this subject! Simply replace regular flour with an equal quantity of an all-purpose or custom blend of gluten-free flours. Be sure to follow the ratio of the ingredients in the original recipe so that you include the same amount of fat, sugar, and liquid. This ratio determines whether you will have a scone, a cookie or a yeast bread. I call this Recipe DNA. Unless you want mutant muffins, stick to the formula in the original recipe. (Yeast breads are the exception.) Experiment. Everything in baking is about the balance of wet to dry ingredients. The more you bake, the better you will become at instinctively knowing when the dough or batter looks right and when it needs more flour or liquid. When you reach that point, you will know how to gently tweak the ratios without creating a monster.

What are your top three favorite types of recipes to bake and why? It depends on my mood. If I read a recipe or hear about a dish that a mainstream chef has created, my taste buds perk up and I want to make it over so I can eat it. Honestly, I bake for myself first. But, once I taste something I like, I want to share it!

Can you tell us about amaranth flour? What kind of texture does it impart to baked goods and what type of recipes do you like to use it in? Amaranth flour is a storehouse of nutrients, protein and fiber. The protein adds more elasticity to gluten-free baked goods than any other flour I have used. That makes it ideal for foods that need that stretch: pie crust, dumpling wrappers, pasta, pizza pockets, croissant, and the pseudo puff pastry dough that I use in the cookbook. The flour is very fine so there is no grittiness. It produces light, delicate layer cakes. However, amaranth does have a slight aftertaste so I use only 25 percent amaranth in a gluten-free blend. It's just enough to add elasticity without defining the taste. Store amaranth flour in the refrigerator as it goes rancid quickly.

What kind of gluten-free recipes would you suggest for a beginner to start with? Begin with simple recipes for muffins, cookies or scones. Before trying a from-scratch recipe for a yeast bread, pie crust, or pizza, make up a commercial mix so you have some idea of how the dough should behave.

What's the most challenging recipe you ever developed and why? Grandma's Babka and My Best Carrot Cake in my cookbook are masterpieces. Each took 6 trials to perfect. When going from a gluten-containing recipe to a gluten-free one, the balance of wet to dry was way off. The first carrot cake I made was too oily and sugary. I wanted a light texture, not a soggy one so I cut back on both ingredients little by little. Grandma's Babka reminded me of how differently wheat and gluten-free flours absorb liquids. The original recipe called for 7 cups of flour for 4½ cups of milk. I ended up using 4½ cups of flour blend and 1½ cups of milk.

Do you bake by weight or volume? I use both. When I prepare a flour blend, I weigh out the ingredients in grams. I multiply the weights by however many recipes I want to make. This way the formula is consistent. Once you have a formula, it doesn't matter

if you make five, 50 or 5,000 pounds. But you can't use that method if substituting one flour for another as the weights will vary.

What do you generally use as egg replacers in baking? I use flax gel or pureed silken tofu to replace eggs when they are used as a binder in a recipe. Occasionally I use unsweetened applesauce plus ½ teaspoon baking powder per egg I am replacing. Applesauce adds moisture to baked goods and the pectin is an excellent binder. However, because of the added moisture, this ingredient is a bit of a wild card and the baking time will be longer. I have not had great success using a commercial egg replacer for this purpose. When 1 or 2 teaspoons of egg replacer is called for in a recipe, it is serving as a leavening agent. Instead, I use a teaspoon (or up to 2 teaspoons) of baking powder.

What kind of dairy free replacements do you like to bake with? Do you think the changes affect the texture and flavor? Dairy adds protein to baked goods. It also tenderizes the dough. Some dairy-free replacements are high in protein and I lean toward those as my first preference —soy milk, almond milk, and hemp milk. Vans'e Dairi-Free, often used by people who are casein-free, and rice milk work but neither contains protein. I find that Dairi-Free and rice milk make the final product a bit more dry and brittle.

Chapter 5

Garbanzo Bean Flour

....

a.k.a. chickpea, besan, gram, cici or chana flour

Garbanzo bean flour is one of the most frequently used flours in gluten-free baking; it's the all-purpose superstar. It's high in protein and allows recipes to rise by providing structure. This gives baked goods their shape and form. Because of this, it is a wonderful flour for making bread, which is why we have six different bread recipes in this chapter. Garbanzo bean flour has a strong flavor that subsides when it is baked. We've discovered that in isolation, this flavor can be off-putting to some. It works best when used with other flours. We like to use garbanzo bean flour in savory recipes or sweet recipes that have equally strong flavors to soften the bean flavor.

A Note on Garfava Flour:

Garfava flour is a mix of garbanzo bean flour and fava bean flour. It is similar in taste and texture to garbanzo bean flour and can be used the same way.

Nutritional Highlights:

This high fiber flour is a nutritional power-house. It has been shown to support healthy digestive tract function, reduce the risk of heart disease, and can aid in blood glucose regulation.

Brand Comparison:

The quality of the various garbanzo bean flour brands that we tested was all very similar. However, we found we preferred Dakota Prairie flour. Ground incredibly fine, it out-performed the others by giving us an extra tall rise in our bread recipes. Finely ground flour is always your best bet in gluten-free baking. By using it, you will avoid gritty baked goods. All of Dakota Prairie's Flours are high quality and very finely ground.

Best flours to substitute for garbanzo bean flour:

We don't recommend substituting garbanzo bean flour for other flours in bread recipes. Its high protein content helps bread to rise and other flours are not likely to work as well. If you can't get your hands on any garbanzo bean flour then soy flour is the next best option for breads as it has the second highest protein content of the gluten-free flours.

Sorghum and Quinoa Flour:

For other non-bread recipes, garbanzo flour works similar in texture to sorghum or quinoa flour and shou8ld be used in a 1:1 ratio.

Teff, Millet, Brown Rice, and White Rice Flour:

These flours also can be substituted in a 1:1 ratio. However, they will change the texture.

Buckwheat Flour:

Can be subbed 1:1, however buckwheat is really only best as a replacement for recipes that are meant to be dense (like brownies).

Garbanzo Bean Flour Tips:

- This is a versatile flour. Can be used in almost any type of recipe.

- One of the best flours for making bread due to its high level of protein. This flour formed the best air pockets in our bread recipes and mimicked gluten-containing bread the most. The higher the percentage of garbanzo bean flour we used, the lighter and fluffier our bread became.

- Works best when combined with other flours.

- Ignore the strong flavor of your batters; it will dissipate drastically as it bakes.

- Can reduce the number of eggs needed in a recipe due to its high protein content.

Garlic Cheese Bread

• •

We love using Daiya cheese for this bread, although if you can tolerate dairy, go ahead and use your favorite brand of cheddar cheese. If you prefer not to use either, just bake without the cheese and then dip in marinara sauce. Your family will love it!

Yield: One 10 x 14 inch rectangle

DIRECTIONS:

1. In a large bowl, whisk together the garbanzo bean flour, brown rice flour, tapioca starch, baking powder, Italian seasoning, and salt. Set aside.

3. In a medium-sized bowl, stir the water, yeast and honey. Let sit for 5 minutes to proof. The yeast should start bubbling on top.

4. Once the yeast is done proofing, put the eggs, psyllium whole husks, apple cider vinegar, and oil in a large bowl. Beat with an electric beater on low speed until well mixed, then add the yeast and water, then slowly add in the flour. Once the flour is all mixed in, turn the speed up to medium and beat for 5 minutes. It will be like a thick batter.

5. Let dough rise in a steam box for 30 minutes.

6. Preheat oven to 400 degrees F. Pour batter out onto a greased cookie sheet and spread thin (about 10 x 14 inches). You can wet your fingers to do this since it will be really sticky. Sprinkle grated cheese and garlic on top. Bake for 20 minutes. Serve hot from the oven.

Best when eaten warm out of the oven. Leftovers can be frozen and reheated.

INGREDIENTS:

57 grams garbanzo bean flour (½ lightly filled cup)

65 grams brown rice flour (½ lightly filled cup)

60 grams tapioca starch (½ cup)

2 teaspoons baking powder

1 tablespoon Italian seasoning

¾ teaspoon salt

1 cup lukewarm water

1 packet quick rise yeast (2¼ teaspoons)

2 teaspoons honey

2 eggs (room temperature)*

¼ cup whole psyllium husks (ground ctip hia seeds will not work)

1 teaspoon apple cider vinegar

1 tablespoon olive oil

2 cloves garlic, minced

1 cup grated cheddar cheese

Tip: If your eggs aren't at room temperature put them in a bowl filled with hot tap water and let sit until ready to use.

Caramelized Onion & Tomato Soufflé with Pumpkin Bread

. . . .

The traditional soufflé gets a makeover in this homey rendition. Caramelized onions and tomatoes meld in a savory soufflé that's topped and baked with scoops of pumpkin bread batter. The result is a comforting dish perfect for a cozy autumn dinner or crisp spring brunch.

Yield: 9 servings

DIRECTIONS:

1. Preheat oven to 375 degrees F. Lightly oil an 8 x 8 inch baking dish.

2. Heat the olive oil in a small pan over medium low heat. Add the onions and pour ¾ teaspoon of salt over them. Let them cook for 5 minutes, stirring occasionally. Add the garlic, oregano, sage, nutmeg, and honey. Cook for 10 minutes, stirring occasionally. Take off heat and put into a large bowl.

3. Whisk the onions, 3 eggs, and 1 cup of milk together. Pour into baking dish. Top with sliced tomatoes. Put in oven and bake for 10 minutes.

4. While the soufflé begins to bake, start on your pumpkin bread batter. In a medium-sized bowl, stir together the flaxseed meal, psyllium husks, water, honey, olive oil, pumpkin puree, and 1 egg yolk (put egg white aside in a large mixing bowl).

5. In another medium-sized mixing bowl, whisk together the garbanzo bean flour, tapioca starch, potato starch, baking powder, and salt.

6. With an electric beater, beat the egg white in the large bowl until soft peaks form. Beat in the flax seed mix, then the dry ingredients. Continue to beat for 5 minutes on medium speed.

7. When the soufflé has baked for 10 minutes, take baking dish out and scoop dollops of the batter over the soufflé. It's okay to have empty spaces in between scoops because the bread will rise and spread. Place the dish back in the oven and bake for 35 minutes or until a knife inserted into the bread portion comes out clean.

Serve warm from the oven.

INGREDIENTS:

SOUFFLÉ:

1 tablespoon extra virgin olive oil

½ medium yellow onion, thinly sliced

¾ teaspoon salt

1 large garlic clove, minced

½ teaspoon dried oregano

¼ teaspoon dried sage

⅛ teaspoon ground nutmeg

1 tablespoon honey

3 large eggs

1 cup milk

2 medium tomatoes, sliced in thin rounds

PUMPKIN BREAD:

1 tablespoon ground flax seed meal

1 tablespoon whole psyllium husks

1 tablespoon boiling water

1 tablespoon honey

1 tablespoon olive oil

¼ cup unsweetened pumpkin puree

1 large egg, separated

42 grams garbanzo bean flour (¼ lightly filled cup plus 2 tablespoons)

13 grams tapioca starch (2 tablespoons)

16 grams potato starch (1½ tablespoons)

1 tablespoon double acting baking powder

½ teaspoon salt

Blueberry Oat Mini Muffins with Walnut Streusel

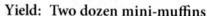

These mini delights are a lovely way to start your morning. Filled with protein and fiber, and low in sugar, you'll feel comfortable feeding them to your family for breakfast. They also freeze well for those days when you just need something to grab on your way out the door.

Yield: Two dozen mini-muffins

DIRECTIONS:

1. Preheat the oven to 375 degrees F. Grease two 12-cup mini-muffin tins.

2. In your food processor, blend the streusel ingredients until crumbly. Set aside.

3. In a large bowl, whisk together the garbanzo bean flour, brown rice flour, tapioca starch, oats, sugar, baking powder, baking soda, xanthan gum, salt, and cinnamon.

4. In a medium-sized bowl, whisk the eggs, oil, applesauce, milk, vanilla, and lemon juice. Stir the wet ingredients into the dry. Fold in the blueberries. Scoop into mini-muffin tins and pat the streusel topping over each one. Bake for 12 minutes or until a knife inserted in the middle comes out clean.

INGREDIENTS:

STREUSEL:

1 date

¼ cup walnuts

1 tablespoon unrefined granulated sugar

25 grams certified gluten-free rolled oats (¼ cup)

MUFFINS:

86 grams garbanzo bean flour (¾ lightly filled cup)

65 grams brown rice flour (½ lightly filled cup)

90 grams tapioca starch (¾ cup)

75 grams cup certified gluten-free rolled oats (¾ cup)

¼ cup unrefined granulated sugar

1 teaspoon baking powder

1 teaspoon baking soda

1 teaspoon xanthan gum

1 teaspoon salt

½ teaspoon cinnamon

2 large eggs

⅓ cup mild flavored oil

½ cup unsweetened applesauce

¾ cup milk

1 teaspoon pure vanilla extract

½ teaspoon lemon juice

¾ cup blueberries

Chickpea Scallion Bread

This is a hearty bread, high in fiber and protein, with a subtle nutty flavor. We love serving it for a special dinner, then slicing the leftovers to enjoy as our morning toast throughout the week. As with our other yeast recipes, this requires a steam box.

Yield: One 9 x 5 inch loaf

DIRECTIONS:

1. Grease a 9 x 5 inch bread pan.

2. In a medium-sized bowl, whisk together the garbanzo bean flour, white rice flour, potato starch, yeast and salt. Set aside.

3. In a small bowl, stir together the flax seed meal, psyllium husks, 2 tablespoons plus 2 teaspoons of water, and oil. Puree the chickpeas with 5 tablespoons of water. Stir the chickpea puree and scallions into the flax mix. Set aside.

4. In a large bowl, beat the eggs on high until they become foamy. Add the sugar and continue to beat on high for 5 minutes. Beat in the flax mixture on medium until it is completely mixed in. Slowly pour in the flour, continuing to beat, until the batter is completely mixed. Scoop batter into the bread pan. It will be closer to a pancake batter than traditional bread dough. Brush oil on top.

5. Put the pan in a steam box. Let it rise for 1 hour or until it is level with the top of the pan. Once it has risen, preheat the oven to 375 degrees F.

6. Bake for 45 minutes. Let cool for a few minutes before turning onto a cooling rack. Let cool completely before cutting.

Slice bread and store in an airtight container in the fridge or freeze for later use.

Note: You can use a smaller baking pan but don't let it rise too long. You just want it to rise to the top of the pan. Also, baking time may vary slightly with a smaller pan.

INGREDIENTS:

86 grams garbanzo bean flour (¾ lightly filled cups)

78 grams white rice flour (½ lightly filled cup)

86 grams potato starch (½ cup)

1 package quick rise yeast (2¼ teaspoons)

¾ teaspoon salt

¼ cup ground flax seed meal

¼ cup whole psyllium husks

¼ cup plus 2 tablespoons lukewarm water

2 tablespoons plus 2 teaspoons olive oil

1 cup canned chickpeas, rinsed and drained

5 tablespoons lukewarm water

1 scallion, finely chopped

4 large eggs (room temperature)*

¼ cup unrefined granulated sugar

Italian Herb Crackers

Buying gluten-free crackers at the store can get expensive. We like to make these crackers to have on hand for snacking. We love the Italian spices, but you can always adjust the herbs to your own preference.

Yield: Four servings

DIRECTIONS:

1. Preheat oven to 350 degrees F. Set aside two cookie sheets.

2. In a large bowl, whisk together garbanzo bean flour, brown rice flour, tapioca starch, flax seeds, herbs, salt, baking soda, and baking powder. Set aside.

3. In a medium-sized bowl, pour boiling water over flax seed meal and psyllium husks. Stir together, then stir in olive oil and lemon juice.

4. Stir wet ingredients into the dry, then knead until a ball of dough is formed. Cut the dough in half and roll one half as thinly as possible between two pieces of parchment paper.

5. Cut slices in it for whatever shape you prefer your crackers to be. Don't worry about having ragged edges (it gives them a nice rustic appearance), but make sure to cut large enough crackers that you can dip them or add a spread or cheese.

6. Place the dough on the parchment paper on a cookie sheet. Set aside and repeat with the other piece of dough. Bake for 22-25 minutes, checking after 22 minutes. They should be crispy but not turning brown. Take parchment paper off cookie sheet to cool.

Store in an airtight container at room temperature.

INGREDIENTS:

- 86 grams garbanzo bean flour (¾ lightly filled cup)
- 65 grams brown rice flour (½ lightly filled cup)
- 60 grams tapioca starch (½ cup)
- ¼ cup whole flax seeds
- 1 tablespoon dried basil
- 1 tablespoon dried parsley
- 2 teaspoons dried marjoram
- 1 teaspoon dried oregano
- 1 teaspoon salt
- ½ teaspoon baking soda
- ½ teaspoon baking powder
- 1 tablespoon ground flax seed meal
- 1 tablespoon whole psyllium husks
- ½ cup boiling water
- 5 tablespoons olive oil
- 1 teaspoon fresh lemon juice

Artisan Sandwich Bread

Making a big, beautiful loaf of gluten-free bread is 100 percent possible. You will be delighted with the air pockets, soft texture and perfect crust of this bread. The garbanzo bean flour, eggs, and xanthan gum make this possible through their ability to provide structure. Don't make any alterations and pull out your kitchen scale for this one.

Yield: One 9 x 5 inch loaf

DIRECTIONS:

1. Place 2 large glasses of water into your microwave. Turn the microwave on and run it for 15-20 minutes while you are preparing the bread dough. This will create a warm and humid proofing box. Run the microwave just until the bread pan is ready to go in.

2. In a cup or bowl, combine the warm water, yeast and 1 tablespoon of granulated sugar. Set aside to proof 5-10 minutes.

3. Use a mixer to beat the eggs until they begin to froth and bubble some. Add the 2 tablespoons of sugar and oil, and continue to beat.

4. Add the rice flour, garbanzo bean flour, potato starch, xanthan gum, baking powder, and salt. Pour in the proofed yeast/water mixture.

5. Stir the mixture by hand until very well combined. Dough will resemble a very thick sticky cake batter.

6. Grease a large 9 x 5 inch bread pan. Pour the bread batter into the prepared pan. Smooth surface with a greased spatula. Draw a line down the center to give bread its characteristic look. It's important to get the dough as smooth as possible. Lumps will be exaggerated when the bread bakes.

7. Quickly place the loaf into the humid microwave, keeping the door open as short a period as possible. If the door has been open too long and the humidity escapes, turn the microwave back on with the bread in it for about 10 seconds.

8. Set a timer and allow the bread to proof in the microwave (keeping the microwave off) for 30 minutes. Do not open the microwave during this time. Meanwhile preheat the oven to 375 degrees F.

9. After the 30 minutes, quickly move the proofed loaf into the hot oven. Bake at 375 degrees F for 18 minutes. Turn down to 350 degrees F and bake for another 28-30 minutes.

10. Keep an eye on the bread; after the first 18 minutes you may want to tent it with aluminum foil. Wait until after this 18 minutes as you do not want to prevent the bread from rising. The darker the outside becomes the crustier it will be. This can be adjusted to your preference.

11. Remove from oven and allow the bread to cool before removing from the pan and slicing.

Note: This bread, like most gluten-free breads, has the best texture when it is slightly warm. Once it has cooled, store it in sealed bag or slice and freeze for another day's use.

INGREDIENTS:

158 grams warm water (about ⅔ cup)

10 grams fast acting yeast (1 tablespoon)

17 grams sugar (do not use palm sugar or xylitol) (1 tablespoon)

3 large eggs

30 grams granulated sugar (2 tablespoons)

51 grams oil (4 tablespoons)

123 grams superfine white rice flour (1 lightly filled cup)

58 grams garbanzo bean flour (½ lightly filled cup)

121 grams potato starch (⅔ cup)

11 grams xanthan gum (1 tablespoon)

11 grams double acting baking powder (1 tablespoon)

½ teaspoon salt

Egg Challah

This challah is made possible by garbanzo bean flour. It provides unbelievable structure and in turn this loaf will rise to great heights in the first 15 minutes of its baking time. Using a baking pan provides the structure needed to make this soft and fluffy bread. Following the gram measurements will Yield the very best results.

Yield: One 9 x 5 inch loaf

DIRECTIONS:

1. Combine the lukewarm water, yeast and sugar in a small bowl. Mix and set aside to proof.

2. Place a large cup of water in your microwave and turn the microwave on for 15 minutes. Run the microwave while you are preparing the bread dough. Keep running it just until you place the bread in.

3. Vigorously beat the 2 large eggs. Once they have become frothy and are bubbly, add the sugar and then the oil. Continue to beat on high until it begins to thicken slightly.

4. Add the proofed water/yeast/sugar mixture. (It has proofed once it has a head of foam.) Beat in. Add in the rice flour, garbanzo bean flour, potato starch, xanthan gum, baking powder, and salt. Mix well; it will be a very sticky dough.

5. Place the dough into a large oiled 9 x 5 inch bread pan. Dip a spatula in oil and smooth out the surface of the dough as much as possible. Brush half of the egg glaze on.

6. Quickly place the prepared pan into the humid and warm microwave for 30 minutes (do not cover it), leaving the bowl of boiling water in the microwave with it. If you feel a lot of the warm air has escaped, you may turn the microwave on for 10 seconds but no longer. The goal here is to create a warm, moist environment, not cook the dough.

7. While the bread is proofing in the microwave, preheat the oven to 375 degrees F.

8. After 30 minutes of proofing, quickly move the bread pan into the oven. Bake for 15 minutes. Brush the bread with the second ½ of the egg glaze. Turn the oven down to 325 degrees F and bake for another 25 minutes. If the bread begins to brown too much, tent it with a sheet of aluminum foil.

9. Remove from oven and allow to cool before slicing.

Note: Store in a sealed bag to maintain its moisture or freeze for another day.

INGREDIENTS:

147 grams lukewarm water (⅔ cup)

1 tablespoon fast acting yeast

1 tablespoon sugar

2 large eggs

⅓ cup granulated sugar (any variety, though white cane sugar works best)

4 tablespoons oil

100 grams superfine white rice flour (¾ packed cup + 1 tablespoon)

103 grams garbanzo bean flour (¾ packed cup + 1 tablespoon)

132 grams potato starch (⅔ cup + 2 tablespoons)

1 tablespoon xanthan gum

1 tablespoon double acting baking powder

½ teaspoon salt

EGG GLAZE:

1 large egg whisked with 1 tablespoon water

Breakfast Carrot Cake

· ·

We love topping this hearty breakfast cake with our cashew cream frosting. While the frosting can be made with any fruit, bananas and strawberries are our favorite flavors.

Yield: One 8 x 8 inch cake

DIRECTIONS:

1. Preheat the oven to 325 degrees F. Grease an 8 x 8 inch baking pan.

2. Grate the carrots and set aside.

3. In a large bowl, whisk together the potato starch, garbanzo bean flour, white rice flour, baking powder, baking soda, xanthan gum, salt, cinnamon, and sugar.

4. In a medium-sized bowl, stir together the coconut milk, apple cider vinegar, oil, and vanilla extract. Pour the wet ingredients into the dry, stirring completely.

5. Stir in the carrots. Spoon batter into the baking dish and bake for 45 minutes, or until a toothpick inserted in the middle comes out clean. When done, let sit for a few minutes before turning onto a cooling rack. Cool completely before frosting.

Best when eaten on the first day, but can be stored in an airtight container in the fridge or frozen for later use.

INGREDIENTS:

1¼ cup, packed, finely grated carrots (about 4-5 medium carrots)

172 grams potato starch (1 cup)

58 grams garbanzo bean flour (½ lightly filled cup)

78 grams white rice flour (½ lightly filled cup)

1 teaspoon baking powder

1 teaspoon baking soda

1 teaspoon xanthan gum

½ teaspoon salt

½ teaspoon cinnamon

¾ cup unrefined granulated sugar

¾ cup full-fat canned coconut milk

1 teaspoon apple cider vinegar

⅓ cup mild flavored oil

1 teaspoon vanilla extract

Ask the Expert

. . . .

Amy Green understands the ins and outs of sugar-free baking better than most. She has been eating gluten- and sugar-free since 2004, and has become an inspiration to many with her blog and cookbook, *Simply Sugar & Gluten-Free: 180 Recipes You Can Make in 20 Minutes or Less.*

How long have you been baking gluten-free? I've been gluten-free since August of 2007, but I didn't bake until I met my husband. It really wasn't a priority until I met Joe and then I wanted to learn how to cook for him.

Do you remember the first thing you ever baked gluten-free? I made a Black Forest Cake, and it just flopped. I worked really hard on it and I remember standing in the middle of my kitchen crying. But the first successful thing I made was a carrot cupcake, which is on my blog and is still one of my most popular recipes.

What are the top things every new gluten-free baker should know?
1. Don't plan your meal around a baked good. When you start baking gluten-free, it's smart to do it when you have time to experiment. If your meal is a pot pie and it flops, you're going to be disappointed.

2. Understand that the flours are not going to work the way you expect them to. They're going to behave very differently than wheat flour and it will take time to understand them.

Do you have any money saving tips for gluten-free bakers?
- Know how to store your flours (this information is often on the bag). If there are flours you don't use as often, store them in the freezer.

- Get creative with your leftovers. You can always freeze breads, scones and quick breads, and use them later to make bread pudding.

- Be smart about where you get your recipes from. Go to a source that you know has been tested.

What tips would you give for someone wanting to convert a family favorite recipe to gluten-free? When converting from non gluten-free, I read the recipe through first. If it calls for 1½ cups of white flour, I start with 1½ cups of my all-purpose blend. I know how that works, so that's my go-to starting off point. Then take it from there. Make one change at a time. If you change six things at once, the recipe might not work out right. And this way, you know which ingredient caused the problem.

Also, think about the product you want to make. Is the structure dense or light and fluffy? Look at the quality of the individual flours, and choose which flours to use based on that. It's the same with wheat baking (you can use whole wheat, white, bread flour, semolina, etc.). In this case, you just have a lot of different choices, and their uses are not clearly designated.

What are your top three favorite flours to work with and why? I like buckwheat flour because it has an earthy taste, behaves more like wheat than a lot of the other flours, and is nutritious. Garfava bean flour is easy to use as part of a blend because it's higher in protein and adds structure to baked good. It's also high in nutrients. And sorghum is easy to use and is high in antioxidants.

What differences have you noticed between garbanzo bean and garfava flour? Garfava is milder in taste, so I prefer it for baked goods. Once it's baked, you can't taste the beany taste. I've never actually used it on its own because it needs the other flavors to balance it out.

What kind of gluten-free recipes would you suggest for a beginner to start with? Start with one from a trusted source, one that has been tested and you know it works. Quick breads and muffins are the easiest to start with.

What's the most challenging recipe you developed and why? Frosting has been the most difficult because I don't use white sugar. But I've finally developed a buttercream recipe I love that's free of refined sugars. Bread recipes are also challenging. I use baker's ratios to troubleshoot and figure out percentages of different ingredients.

Is there one recipe that has left you stumped after all these years? There hasn't been anything I haven't been able to eventually troubleshoot. There are things I haven't attempted yet, like learning how to use coconut flour. I've had lots of failures though; I spent a long time failing at gluten-free baking before I ever succeeded. And even now I still have flops, and I just try it again. My sourdough bread is fabulous, but it took a lot of playing around with it and getting the right ratios together to make it work.

Do you bake by weight or volume? When I do my breads, I bake by weight because that's how the baker's percentages work, by weight. With other things, I typically bake by volume because I'm not making a mass quantity. It takes more time when putting a recipe together to stop and weigh as I go. I love using coconut oil, but it has a lower melting point than butter or shortening so it will act a bit differently in the oven.

What differences have you noticed between tapioca starch, potato starch, and arrowroot starch? Tapioca is less dense and has less thickening power than arrowroot. Arrowroot can be used in place of tapioca starch, and has some soothing effects on the gut, but it is so much more expensive. It's great for sauces if you know how to use it.

Potato starch is dense and thickens well. I like to use a combination of tapioca and potato starch in my all-purpose blend because it thickens and lightens at the same time. This makes it more like a traditional wheat product so that I can serve it to people who don't usually eat gluten-free and they will love it.

Can you give our readers some gluten-free bread making tips? Are there certain flours or other ingredients that you always use when making bread? In the Great Depression, they added fava bean flour to the wheat flour to make it cheaper without affecting the structure. I use garfava bean mix in my breads to give them structure. One of the things I've noticed is that gluten-free breads are often wet or gummy inside, so it's a matter of getting everything balanced so you have that traditional texture that still tastes good. Also, people have wild expectations of bread and all baked goods in general. They want them to last for three weeks. We know gluten-free products typically have a shorter shelf life than wheat, and people need to have realistic expectations. Bread molds. People are just used to buying food with preservatives in it.

Is there anything else you think our readers should know about gluten-free baking? Start with one flour blend, and keep it very simple in the beginning. Once you've developed a comfort level with that, expand and branch out. The more you do it, the more you get that intuitive feel for it and the easier it gets. And it really is fun, and it becomes very easy!

Fun uses for garbanzo bean flour

· ·

- Used to make socca, a thin, unleavened pancake
- Can be rehydrated to make hummus
- Used to thicken sauces or soups

Chapter 6

Coconut Flour

The reason we wrote these books was because of coconut flour. We coined it the mystery flour as we both struggled to fully understand how it worked. There was very little information available. We found lots of recipes, but not an explanation of how to use the flour. For two recipe developers hungry for new ideas, this proved to be an opportunity to help others feeling just as frustrated as we were. We hope the following tips and recipes will provide a strong enough understanding so you too can step into your kitchen and give this flour a try!

This fibrous flour can be light and fluffy or extremely dense. Eggs are the magical elixir to baking with it. Eggs lift the flour and act as the binding agent holding all the ingredients together. Coconut flour has another unique characteristic when liquid is added: it absorbs three times more liquid than other flours. This may fool you into thinking that it's super absorbent. However, this is not the case. When your baked good is put into the oven, the flour will suddenly refuse to absorb the additional liquid. You'll notice at the end of the bake time that the exterior of your baked good is hard, with an oddly developed tough skin, while the inside is undercooked. This brings us back to the eggs. Not only do the eggs lift and bind, but they also absorb the extra moisture. Let's try an example: Mix a tablespoon of coconut flour with a few tablespoons of water in a bowl. Once mixed, add it to a pre-heated skillet and cook like a pancake. You will notice that, regardless of the time in the skillet, the mixture will not dry out. Now lets repeat this example by adding an egg. Success! A nice little pancake.

Baking without eggs is possible but starch must be added. All the gluten-free flours, especially the starches (tapioca, arrowroot and potato starch), have the ability to act as an egg substitute. Just as the egg does, they will bind the coconut flour together and dry out the moisture when baked. However, understand that these starches are not a magical substitution and it may take some iteration to get your intended results. It is more difficult to achieve a desirable airy texture without the use of eggs. We suggest combining starch, another flour and leavening agents to do so. One of our favorite all-purpose blends uses a 1:1:1 ratio (cups, not grams) of coconut flour to white rice flour to tapioca starch. This blend can be used cup for cup in most egg-free, gluten-free recipes that call for an all-purpose mix, and has a mildly sweet flavor.

Nutritional Highlights
High in dietary fiber and protein, coconut flour may be beneficial in the proper management of blood glucose control, as well as in the prevention of chronic diseases such as diabetes mellitus, heart disease, and cancer.

Brand Comparison:
There are many great coconut flours on the market today. We've worked with several brands with varying levels of success. Bob's Red Mill and Let's Do...Organic are widely available, good quality flours. However, our personal favorite comes from Nuts.com.

- Best flours to substitute for coconut flour: None. Coconut flour is like no other. If a recipe calls for a small amount, try substituting a variety of flours or starches. However, if the coconut flour is an integral recipe ingredient we suggest using it. And remember that coconut flour absorbs extra liquid in the mixing bowl, so if you sub in another flour, you may need less liquid overall.

If you have a recipe that uses another flour, and you want to add in some coconut flour, we recommend substituting a small amount of coconut flour for the other flour (10 to 20 percent of the total amount of flour), and adding an equal amount of liquid.

A frequent question we get asked is whether almond and coconut flour can be used interchangeably. The answer is a resounding no! They work very differently in recipes.

Coconut flour tips:
- Coconut flour has a cloyingly sweet, strong flavor. In small doses it adds great flavor to recipes (even just 1-2 tablespoons will do). If using a large amount, you may notice the sweet flavor and coconut undertones.

- Four to six eggs are needed per cup of coconut flour. This will range based on the type of recipe you are trying to create.

- Small amounts of liquid sweeteners, such as honey, coconut nectar, brown rice syrup or molasses, can help bind coconut flour recipes.

- You may find that your cake, pancake and muffin batters using coconut flour are on the thick side. This is to ensure the recipes cook all the way through.

- Almond flour and coconut flour work well together. Adding coconut flour to almond creates a hearty texture with a bit more chew. The almond flour acts as the binding and moistening agent, allowing the coconut flour to flourish.

- We designed our recipes to work without sifting the coconut flour (we like to keep things simple), but often you can get a slightly lighter result if you sift your flour first.

- As coconut flour sometimes has the tendency to clump, we suggest using a mixer to sufficiently beat your ingredients together.

Coconut flour does not behave well in yeast recipes when it is the exclusive flour. It requires another grain or starch to activate the yeast. Even still, we do not suggest combining it with yeast and starch as the heaviness of the flour may weight down your baked goods.

The texture of coconut flour works great without the use of other flours in pancake, cake, cupcake, muffin, cookie, and scone recipes with eggs. When starch is added, it can make incredibly soft and fluffy baked goods. Our Peanut Butter Pancake Recipe is a great example of this.

Fun uses for coconut flour

- Replace breadcrumbs in meatballs. We like to add approximately one tablespoon to most recipes calling for about a pound of meat.
- Coconut flour can be used to dredge meat prior to cooking.
- You can add coconut flour to smoothies for added fiber.
- Coconut flour can be used in small amounts in frosting recipes to give them some extra body.

Peanut Butter Pancakes

These pancakes are extraordinarily soft and airy with the perfect amount of peanut butter flavor. Layer them up with jelly for an out-of-this-world experience. We assure you that you will feel inspired to test this particular flour and egg combination in other recipe applications; think fluffy cake!

Yield: One dozen pancakes

DIRECTIONS:

1. Combine the eggs and milk in a blender on high speed for 30 seconds.

2. Add all the remaining ingredients and mix on high for another 30 seconds to one minute. The batter will be thick.

3. Heat a non-stick or well-seasoned cast iron skillet with a little oil. Cook the pancakes over medium heat, giving the first side 1 to 2 minutes to cook before flipping. If you find the pancakes are hard to flip, add up to an extra tablespoon of tapioca flour to the batter.

4. Layer jelly in-between pancakes when serving. Drizzle top with additional warmed peanut butter (or nut butter). Try adding crushed peanuts to the batter for an additional crunch.

Note: If you prefer your pancakes less fluffy, cut down on the baking soda or leave it out altogether.

INGREDIENTS:

4 large eggs

200 grams milk (1 cup)

111 grams peanut butter (or other nut/seed butter of choice) (½ cup)

¼-½ cup granulated sugar (any variety)

1 teaspoon baking soda

½ teaspoon salt

67 grams coconut flour (½ lightly filled cup)

28 grams of tapioca or arrowroot starch (3½ tablespoons)

(Grain Free) Breakfast Cookie Bars

INGREDIENTS:

158 grams
   blanched
   almond flour
   (1¼ packed cups)

38 grams coconut
   flour (¼ packed
   cup)

2 tablespoons
   room
   temperature
   butter or
   shortening

4 tablespoons
   granulated sugar
   (any variety)

¼ teaspoon
   baking powder

¼ teaspoon salt

2 large eggs

3 tablespoons milk
   or water

Your favorite thick
   jelly, jam or fruit
   preserves

The combination of coconut and almond flour is a duo we love to use when we bake grain free. The coconut flour in this recipe added some hearty texture to the bars, making them a rustic cross between a cookie and a breakfast bar. Loaded with protein and fiber, this is one happy breakfast.

Yield: 8-10 bars

DIRECTIONS:

1. Preheat oven to 330 degrees F.

2. Mix the almond flour, coconut flour and butter in the bowl of a stand mixer or food processor. Mix in remaining ingredients.

3. Dust a sheet of parchment paper with almond flour. Place the ball of dough on a floured surface. Add additional almond flour as needed to prevent sticking. Gently roll out the dough into a ¼-½ inch thick rectangle.

4. Cover the dough with a thick layer of jelly, leaving a border around the edges.

5. Using the parchment paper as your guide, lift half the dough and place on top of other side creating a smaller rectangle. Use the sheet of parchment to gently seal the edges with your hands. Slice the dough into bars. Place them on a cookie sheet.

6. Bake 20-25 minutes until edges become golden.

Note: Try filling these bars with various nuts and seeds along with the fruit. Rolling the stuffed dough into pinwheel cookies is another fun option.

Store in an airtight container at room temperature or freeze for later use.

Curry Scones

··

These savory scones can be served at dinner instead of biscuits or naan. They also make a wonderful accompaniment to Sunday brunch with ginger preserves.

Yield: One dozen scones

DIRECTIONS:

1. Preheat the oven to 400 degrees F. Lightly grease a cookie sheet.

2. Stir the flax seeds, chia seeds, coconut milk, and lemon juice together in a small bowl. Set aside.

3. In a large bowl, whisk together the coconut flour, white rice flour, tapioca starch, sugar, curry, baking powder, baking soda, and salt. Cut in the shortening. Stir in the coconut milk mixture and continue to stir until it's well combined. Use your hands to knead it a few times until it comes together into a dough.

4. Divide the dough into two mounds. Flatten into circular disks on the cookie sheet about an inch high. Cut each disk into 6 triangles. Bake for 15 minutes. Let cool slightly before eating.

Best when eaten fresh from the oven, but leftovers can be frozen and reheated.

INGREDIENTS:

2 tablespoons ground flax seed meal

2 tablespoons ground chia seeds

1¼ cups full-fat canned coconut milk at room temperature

2 teaspoons lemon juice

80 grams coconut flour (⅔ lightly filled cup)

104 grams white rice flour (⅔ lightly filled cup)

80 grams tapioca starch (⅔ cup)

¼ cup unrefined granulated sugar

1 tablespoon curry powder

2 teaspoons double acting baking powder

½ teaspoon baking soda

½ teaspoon salt

½ cup shortening, cold

Cinnamon Raisin Bread

Tried by six of our recipe testers and loved by all, this recipe is a special one. The texture is a cross between yeasted and quick bread. Toast up a slice and enjoy it with a dab of butter.

Yield: One 8.5 x 4.5 inch loaf

DIRECTIONS:

1. Preheat oven to 325 degrees F. Grease a small bread pan (about 8.5 x 4.5 inches).

2. Beat the eggs. Once they are frothy, add the milk, oil and sugar. Continue to beat until combined.

3. Add the remaining ingredients except for the raisins and beat batter until well mixed.

4. Stir in the raisins. Quickly pour the thick batter into the prepared pan. Smooth the top.

5. Bake 70-80 minutes. You may need to cover the pan with aluminum foil during the last 30 minutes of baking.

6. Cool 30 minutes before slicing.

Note: This loaf will not rise significantly in the oven. If not immediately serving, store in a sealed bag at room temperature or freeze for another day.

INGREDIENTS:

8 large eggs

⅓ cup milk

2 tablespoons oil or melted butter

½ cup unrefined granulated sugar

117 grams coconut flour (¾ packed cup)

78 grams flax meal (¾ cup)

2 tablespoons cinnamon

2½ teaspoons double acting baking powder

1 teaspoon vinegar or lemon juice

¼ teaspoon salt

1 cup raisins

Blueberry Buckle

This attractive and delicious cake shows what happens when eggs and coconut flour are combined. The flavor and texture that coconut flour provides shine through in this easy recipe. High in protein and low in carbohydrates, this buckle is healthy to boot

Yield: One 8-inch cake

Directions:

1. Preheat oven to 350 degrees F.

2. Beat eggs. Add remaining ingredients. Beat until well combined. The batter will be thick. Stir in the blueberries.

3. Press into a nonstick 8-inch cake pan.

4. In a separate bowl, make the streusel; combine all ingredients with a fork and sprinkle on top of the buckle.

5. Bake 50-55 minutes. Watch the top of the buckle towards the end. If the streusel begins to get darker than your preference, cover with a sheet of aluminum foil.

If not immediately serving, store covered in the fridge or freeze for another day.

Ingredients:

6 large eggs

121 grams milk (½ cup + 2 tablespoons)

¾ cup granulated sugar (any variety)

1 tablespoons vanilla extract

115 grams coconut flour (1 lightly filled cup)

1 teaspoon double acting baking powder

¼ teaspoon salt

2 cups frozen blueberries

Streusel Topping:

¾ cup unsweetened coconut flakes

⅓ cup granulated sugar (any variety)

1 tablespoon cinnamon

3 tablespoons coconut flour

3 tablespoons mild flavored oil or melted butter

Pinch of salt

Chocolate Chip Waffle Cookies

While we think of these as a dessert and eat them with ice cream although some of our friends enjoy serving them for breakfast. We'll let you decide.

Yield: Four dozen cookies

Directions:

1. Turn your waffle iron on. In a small bowl, mix the flax seed meal, psyllium husks, and ⅔ cup of coconut milk. Set aside.

2. In a medium-sized bowl, whisk the quinoa flakes, coconut flour, white rice flour, potato starch, baking soda, cream of tartar, and salt. Set aside.

3. In a large bowl, beat the shortening, sugar, and ¼ cup of coconut milk until smooth. Beat in the flax seed mixture, then the dry ingredients. Fold in the chocolate chips.

4. Drop by the tablespoon onto a lightly oiled waffle iron. Your waffle cookies might be ready when your waffle iron says it's done, or they may need another minute. You can test this by lifting the iron a few inches. If the cookie looks like it will stick and come apart, let it cook another minute. When it's ready, you should be able to open the iron and take the cookie off with no resistance.

These are best when eaten warm from the iron, but can be stored for days in an airtight container. They can also be frozen and put in your lunchbox in the morning. They will defrost by the time you're ready for lunch and be a nice treat!

Ingredients:

- 3 tablespoons ground flax seed meal
- 1 tablespoon whole psyllium husks or ground chia seeds
- ⅔ cup full-fat canned coconut milk
- 156 grams quinoa flakes (1½ cups)
- 30 grams coconut flour (¼ lightly filled cup)
- 39 grams white rice flour (¼ lightly filled cup)
- 43 grams potato starch (¼ cup)
- ½ teaspoon baking soda
- ¼ teaspoon cream of tartar
- ½ teaspoon salt
- ½ cup shortening
- 1 cup unrefined granulated sugar
- ¼ cup full-fat canned coconut milk
- ¾ cup chocolate chips

Oatmeal Raisin Cookies

· ·

Simple, easy to make, and perfect for a potluck.
Stick with tradition and use raisins or play around
with using chocolate chips, chopped nuts or other
dried fruit.

Yield: Two dozen cookies

DIRECTIONS:

1. In a medium-sized bowl, whisk the oats, coconut flour, rice flour, tapioca starch, baking soda, and salt.

2. In a large bowl, beat the shortening, honey, eggs, and vanilla together on medium speed for 30 seconds. Beat in the flour on low speed until completely mixed. Fold in the raisins.

3. Chill the batter for an hour.

4. Preheat the oven to 350 degrees F. Form balls (about a heaping tablespoon each) and set 2 inches apart onto two lightly greased cookie sheets, 12 per sheet.

5. Bake for 10-12 minutes, until cookies are golden and edges just begin to brown slightly. Remove from the oven and let cool for a few minutes on the cookie sheet before removing to a cooling rack.

Best if eaten fresh from the oven but can be stored in an airtight container in the fridge or frozen for later use.

INGREDIENTS:

154 grams certified gluten-free rolled oats (1½ cups)

30 grams coconut flour (¼ lightly filled cup)

39 grams white rice flour (¼ lightly filled cup)

30 grams tapioca starch (¼ cup)

½ teaspoon baking soda

1 teaspoon salt

½ cup shortening

⅔ cup honey

2 large eggs

2 teaspoons pure vanilla extract

⅔ cup raisins

Cranberry Orange Cake

We love serving this cake without frosting for brunch or adding frosting to turn it into a birthday cake. It pairs nicely with Coconut Cream Frosting.

Yield: One 8 x 8 inch cake

DIRECTIONS:

1. Preheat the oven to 350 degrees F. Lightly grease an 8 x 8 inch baking dish.

2. In a medium-sized bowl, whisk together the white rice flour, coconut flour, tapioca starch, baking powder, baking soda, salt, nutmeg, and cloves. Set aside.

3. In a small bowl, stir the boiling water into the flax seeds and psyllium husks. Set aside.

4. In a large bowl, whisk together the shortening, honey, applesauce, vanilla, and orange juice. Whisk in the flax mixture. Stir in the flour until completely mixed. Stir in cranberries and orange zest.

5. Pour into baking pan and bake for 40-45 minutes, until a toothpick inserted in the middle comes out clean. Let cool completely before serving. Frost if desired with coconut cream frosting.

Store in an airtight container in the fridge or freeze for later use.

INGREDIENTS:

117 grams white rice flour (¾ lightly filled cup)

60 grams coconut flour (½ lightly filled cup)

60 grams tapioca starch (½ cup)

1 tablespoon double acting baking powder

½ teaspoon baking soda

½ teaspoon salt

¼ teaspoon ground nutmeg

⅛ teaspoon ground cloves

1 tablespoon ground flax seed meal

1 teaspoon whole psyllium husks

3 tablespoons boiling water

½ cup shortening

¾ cup honey

3 tablespoons unsweetened applesauce

2 teaspoons pure vanilla extract

½ cup orange juice

1 cup fresh or frozen (thawed if frozen) cranberries

zest of half a medium orange

Ask the Expert

· ·

Meet Kelly Brozyna, the queen of all things coconut flour. Kelly is the author of *The Spunky Coconut Cookbook* and *The Spunky Coconut Grain-Free Baked Goods and Desserts Cookbook*. Kelly develops gluten-, casein- and refined sugar-free recipes. She works with coconut flour in a way that we think you'll love.

How do you feel coconut flour differs from other flours? Coconut flour is the most unusual of all flours, and it has great texture. It absorbs liquids and expands like no other flour. It's also very difficult to use without eggs.

What type of recipes do you like to use coconut flour in? Everything! I use it in almost all of my baking, and even to thicken coconut buttercream frosting.

What kind of flours do you like to combine coconut flour with? Although you can make anything with just coconut flour and eggs, coconut flour tastes best with some tapioca or arrowroot starch. Then I also like to add almond flour or pureed whole beans. The recipes are richer this way.

Do you have any money saving tips for gluten-free bakers? Yes! Using coconut flour and pureed whole beans for baking is really affordable. If you look at my recipes with coconut flour you will see that a little coconut flour goes a really long way. Pureed whole beans are great for baking. Plus they are so much easier to digest if you soak them and cook them yourself.

What are your favorite types of recipes to bake and why? Lately I've been really into biscotti—making all kinds of flavors like mint chocolate, almond, and nutmeg. I love the crunchiness.

Is there one recipe that has left you stumped after all these years? I'm still working on a fried doughnut recipe. It's the one thing I miss the most.

What do you generally use as egg replacers in baking? I prefer chia seed meal and applesauce to replace eggs, because flax contains phytoestrogens. I use baking soda and apple cider vinegar to get a rise similar to eggs.

What kind of dairy free replacements do you like to bake with? My favorite is ghee, though it is technically dairy. Ghee is butter that has been clarified to remove the casein (protein), lactose and whey. Most people can tolerate ghee, and it's the next closest thing to the taste of butter. My second favorite is soy-free Earth Balance Buttery Spread. Cashew milk is my favorite substitute for cream, and takes seconds to make. It tastes remarkably similar to cream when used in baking and sauces.

Chapter 7

Millet Flour

· ·

Millet is a lightweight whole grain flour with a corn-like flavor. It's reminiscent of the flavor and texture you get from using Bisquick. Think of the soft flaky biscuits or delicious fluffy pancakes that your mom used to make. It rises well and makes your recipes soft and flaky, just like our Blueberry Pancake Popovers, which have a distinct pancake texture. If you were to substitute another flour for the millet in this recipe the flavor and texture becomes more akin to classic popovers. It's a great all-purpose flour that works well on its own and when combined with other flours, and we love to experiment with it to make our recipes distinct.

Nutritional Highlights:
Millet is high in antioxidants, calcium and B vitamins.

Brand Comparison:
We found across the board that the majority of brands were similar, but our favorites were Dakota Prairie and Nuts.com.

Best flours to substitute for millet flour:

Sorghum or White Rice Flour:
Sorghum and white rice flour will give your recipes a similar rise to millet but do not have the characteristic corn flavor and ability to produce flaky baked goods.

Teff, Quinoa, Brown Rice and Garbanzo Bean Flour:
These all rise similarly to millet but they have their own distinct flavors that will dramatically affect the taste of any recipe. The flavor of brown rice is mild, but it will change both the texture and color of your baked goods.

Millet Flour Tips:
- Millet flour tends to go rancid quickly and will develop a bitter aftertaste. We suggest giving your flour a little taste test before using it in your recipes to check for bitterness. Store millet in the freezer to give the flour a longer shelf life and buy in bulk if you use it often.
- Can be used as the sole flour in pancake, biscuit, and cookie recipes with the addition of a starch. For instance, our vegan pancake and waffle guide (found in Part 2 of our guides) calls for 1¼ cups of millet flour to ½ cup of potato starch. The result is a light and fluffy pancake that tastes similar to biscuits.
- In yeast breads, balance millet flour with flours that have a higher protein content to help retain the bread's structure and to prevent collapsing after baking.

Fun uses for millet:

- Millet is delicious in its whole grain form and can be used as a gluten-free replacement for couscous due to its small circular shape.
- The millet grain can be cooked and used in vegetarian bean burgers, lending a sweetness to the overall flavor.
- Millet flour can be used to thicken sauces and soups.

Vegan Pizza Crust

· ·

Being gluten-free doesn't mean you have to go without pizza! This vegan rendition is reminiscent of a whole wheat pizza crust, and is an easy recipe to whip up for dinner. We also love topping it with our Cashew Cream Frosting and fruit to make it a dessert pizza!

Yield: One 12-inch pizza crust

DIRECTIONS:

1. Preheat the oven to 400 degrees F. Take out a baking sheet and cut a piece of parchment paper the size of the sheet.

2. In a small bowl, stir together the flax seed, psyllium husks, boiling water, and olive oil. Let sit for 5 minutes.

3. In a large bowl, whisk together the millet flour, potato starch, baking powder, sugar and salt.

4. Once the flax mixture has rested for 5 minutes, whisk it for 30 seconds, then pour it into the dry ingredients, stirring until it comes together into a dough. It should be easy to handle at this point. Shape into a ball and roll it out on the parchment paper to about ⅛–¼ inch thickness. Place the wax paper on the baking sheet. Bake for 10 minutes.

5. Remove from oven and top however you like. Bake another 10 minutes. Serve hot.

   Freeze and reheat leftovers as you would any other pizza.

INGREDIENTS:

1 tablespoon ground flax seed meal

1 tablespoon whole psyllium husks

¾ cup plus 2 tablespoons boiling water

1½ tablespoons olive oil

96 grams millet flour (¾ lightly filled cup)

86 grams potato starch (½ cup)

1 tablespoon double acting baking powder

2 teaspoons unrefined granulated sugar

¾ teaspoon salt

Your favorite pizza toppings

Blueberry Pancake Popovers

Popovers on Christmas morning are a big tradition in my family. We first enjoyed them served with fresh blueberry jam in Maine on a family vacation years ago at Jordan Pond. This recipe is an ode to that wonderful memory. As the title suggests, these popovers have a bit of a pancake texture that you will be sure to enjoy!

–Brittany

Yield: One dozen muffins

DIRECTIONS:

1. Lightly grease 1 muffin tray (12 cups). Preheat oven to 400 degrees F. with muffin tray in it

2. In a blender combine the eggs, oil, and milk and process on high for 30 seconds.

3. Add all remaining ingredients (except for the blueberries) and process again on high for about 1 minute.

4. Stir in the blueberries (do not turn on the blender again after this point).

5. Remove hot pan from preheated oven. Quickly pour the batter evenly into the 12 cups. Place back in oven.

6. Bake 20 minutes at 400 degrees F. Then turn down the heat to 350 degrees F and bake an additional 20 minutes. (Do not open the oven at any point during this baking process.)

7. After the 40 minutes of baking, remove the pancake popovers from the oven and serve hot with maple syrup.

INGREDIENTS:

4 large eggs

2 tablespoons non-dairy melted butter or oil

1 cup milk

1 teaspoon pure vanilla extract

Zest from 1 lemon (optional)

64 grams millet flour (½ lightly filled cup)

44 grams superfine rice flour (¼ lightly filled cup + 1 tablespoon)

57 grams potato starch (⅓ cup)

¼ teaspoon xanthan gum

¼ teaspoon salt

⅓ cup unrefined granulated sugar

1 cup clean and dry blueberries

Cheesy Skillet Biscuits

Our recipe testers raved about these fluffy yeasted biscuits. Millet flour is the star of this show, as it gives these skillet delights their perfect texture and flavor. For those that need to avoid dairy, any cheese substitute can be used. We especially liked Daiya.

Directions:

1. Combine the lukewarm milk, sugar and yeast in a cup. Set aside and allow it to bubble and froth 5 minutes.

2. In a large bowl, combine the millet flour, rice flour, tapioca starch, xanthan gum, salt, baking powder, garlic and mustard Powder.

3. Add the yeast/milk mixture. Stir in the oil, vinegar and cheese. The batter will be very wet. Stir it for a few minutes. It will thicken just slightly.

4. Oil the skillet. Liberally oil your hands to prevent sticking. Placing heaping tablespoons of the wet and sticky dough into your oiled hands and gently shape the biscuits into round mounds. Place the rounded mounds side by side in the skillet until skillet is filled. Cover skillet with lid.

5. Place the skillet on the stovetop and turn a burner on low heat for 1-2 minutes to just barely heat the pan. This gentle heat will provide the heat to encourage the dough to rise. Do not remove the lid from the skillet. Let the dough sit 15-18 minutes until puffy and risen.

6. After the dough has risen, turn the burner back on to medium-low, keeping the lid on. Cook for 12 minutes.

7. Meanwhile, preheat oven to 350 degrees F. After the 12 minutes on the stovetop, remove the lid from the biscuits and place in preheated oven and bake for 10 minutes.

8. Remove the cooked biscuits from the oven and brush with oil or melted butter. Place the biscuits back in the oven and turn on your broiler. Toast the biscuits under this direct heat for 3 to 4 minutes until just slightly golden.

9. Remove from oven and serve.

Note: For this recipe you will need an oven safe 8-9 inch skillet with a lid.

Ingredients:

- 369 grams lukewarm milk (1½ cups)
- 1 tablespoon granulated sugar
- 2¼ teaspoons fast acting yeast
- 172 grams millet flour (1 packed cup)
- 75 grams superfine white or brown rice flour (½ packed cup)
- 205 grams tapioca starch (1⅓ packed cups)
- 1 teaspoon xanthan gum
- 1 teaspoon salt
- 3½ teaspoons double acting baking powder
- 1 tablespoon garlic powder
- 1 tablespoon ground mustard powder
- 1½ tablespoon oil
- 1½ teaspoons vinegar
- ½ cup shredded cheddar cheese (may use up to ¾ cup)
- 1-2 tablespoons of oil for the skillet

Soft Pretzels

These soft pretzels are surprisingly simple to make, with great flavor and texture. Dare we say they are just as good, if not better than those found at most ball parks? For some fun variation, try wrapping the dough around cooked hotdogs to make pretzel dogs.

Yield: 6-8 pretzels

Directions:

1. Combine the lukewarm water, sugar and yeast in a bowl. Set aside for 5 minutes, allowing the yeast to develop.

2. In a large bowl, combine the millet flour, rice flour, potato starch, salt, xanthan gum, baking powder, and oil. Mix well.

3. Stir in the water/yeast mixture. Stir for 2 minutes, allowing the dough to thicken slightly.

4. Lightly coat hands with oil and divide the dough into 6-8 equal sized balls. Gently roll out each ball of dough on a dry clean surface at least 12 inches long. Criss cross each rope into the classic pretzel shape.

5. Carefully place the shaped pretzels onto a cookie sheet. Brush each with a little oil and cover with a towel and place in a warm location for 20-25 minutes, allowing the dough to rise. We suggest placing the pretzels to rise in a warm oven.

6. After 20 minutes, bring the 10 cups of water and ⅔ cup of baking soda to a boil. Once the pretzels have risen, carefully place one or two at a time into the rapidly boiling water. Boil for 30 seconds, flipping once halfway through. Place the boiled pretzels back on the cookie sheet.

7. Preheat oven to 375 degrees F. Brush each pretzel with melted butter or oil and top with coarse sea salt. Bake 13-15 minutes until golden brown. Serve warm with condiment of choice.

Note: Like most rice-based baked goods, these taste best warm. Keeping these pretzels on the smaller side will make them easier to handle when boiling.

Ingredients:

213 grams lukewarm water (¾ cup plus 3½ tablespoons)

2 teaspoons granulated sugar

1½ teaspoons fast acting yeast

80 grams millet flour (½ packed cup plus 1 tablespoon)

120 grams brown rice flour (¾ packed cup)

165 grams potato starch (1 cup)

½ teaspoon salt

¾ teaspoon xanthan gum

½ teaspoon double acting baking powder

1 teaspoon mild flavored oil

10 cups water

⅔ cup baking soda

Melted butter or oil for brushing pretzels

Coarse sea salt

Oatmeal Cream Pies

Most recipes for oatmeal cookies call for brown sugar. Our soft and chewy take on this classic recipe uses healthier sweeteners, leaving you with less guilt. Why not have two?

Yield: Six pies

DIRECTIONS:

1. Preheat oven to 325 degrees F.

2. Combine all melted butter, Sucanat, molasses, milk, and vanilla extract in a large bowl. Stir in the millet flour, tapioca starch, salt, baking powder, cinnamon, and xanthan gum. Stir in the oats last.

3. Place 12 mounds (a little less than ¼ cup each) of dough on an ungreased cookie sheet. Leave a 1-inch space between each cookie. Bake 15-18 minutes.

4. Remove cookies from oven and let cool.

5. Fill with marshmallow cream using a piping bag.

Note: No piping bag? Make your own by scooping the cream filling into a sealable plastic bag and cutting the corner.

Can be stored in the refrigerator or at room temperature in a sealed container for several days.

INGREDIENTS:

10 tablespoons melted butter or mild flavored oil

1 cup Sucanat or coconut palm sugar

2 tablespoons molasses, maple syrup or honey

6 tablespoons milk

1 teaspoon pure vanilla extract

95 grams millet flour (¾ lightly filled cup)

90 grams tapioca or arrowroot starch (¾ cup)

½ teaspoon salt

¼ teaspoon baking powder

1 teaspoon cinnamon

1 teaspoon xanthan gum

148 grams certified gluten-free rolled oats (1½ cup)

MARSHMALLOW CREAM FILLING:

Use store bought or see our recipe in the frosting section.

Funnel Cake

. . . .

This take on the classic festival treat is easy to make. And you'll only need two flours! We selected millet knowing its flavor would complement the overall taste of this fried treat. Get ready for a fun experience that will impress your friends and family alike.

Yield: Four funnel cakes

Directions:

1. In a heavy bottomed saucepan, add several inches of oil. Turn heat on medium while preparing the batter. The temperature should reach 300 degrees F. when tested with a candy thermometer.

2. In a large bowl, combine all of the funnel cake ingredients. Whisk together until well mixed. Pour mixture into a piping bag.

3. Once oil has heated, pipe the batter into the hot oil, swirling it around in circles. The batter will expand and double in size. Cook about 2 minutes on each side.

4. Remove from hot oil and place on paper towel. Dust with powdered sugar.

Ingredients:

Oil for deep frying

140 grams milk (⅔ cup)

4 tablespoons unrefined granulated sugar

1 tablespoon melted butter or mild flavored oil.

1 large egg

95 grams tapioca starch (¾ cup)

76 grams millet flour (½ packed cup)

½ teaspoon xanthan gum

½ teaspoon salt

1 teaspoon double acting baking powder

Powdered sugar for dusting. Unrefined powdered sugar can be made by placing any type of unrefined granulated sugar into a coffee mill.

Apple Fritters

These babies were a favorite among our recipe testers. Their texture is fluffy, similar to a cake doughnut.

Yield: One dozen

DIRECTIONS:

1. Pour several inches of oil into a heavy bottomed pot and heat it to 325 degrees F.

2. Combine the potato starch, rice flour, millet flour, xanthan gum, baking powder, sugar and salt in a large bowl. Stir well.

3. Add in the egg, milk and oil. Stir until mixture comes together. Stir in the chopped apples. The batter will be relatively thin.

4. Place heaping tablespoons of the batter into the hot oil. Make sure not to overcrowd the pot. The fritters will triple in size. Fry 4-5 minutes, until golden brown. If the fritters do not blow up quickly, the oil may need to be hotter; if the fritters brown too quickly, turn the heat down.

5. Remove from oil and place on a paper towel to cool. Once semi-cooled, coat in powdered sugar and cinnamon.

Note: If the batter is not maintaining its shape in the oil, turn down the heat. Add up to ¼ cup of additional sugar if you prefer your fritters sweeter.

INGREDIENTS:

Oil for deep frying

55 grams potato starch (⅓ cup)

43 grams superfine white rice flour (⅓ packed cup)

55 grams millet flour (⅓ packed cup)

½ teaspoon xanthan gum

1½ teaspoons double acting baking powder

⅓ cup unrefined granulated sugar

¼ teaspoon salt

1 large egg

230 grams milk (1 cup)

1 tablespoon melted butter or mild flavored oil

1 cup chopped apples

Powdered sugar and cinnamon for coating. To make unrefined powdered sugar, just run any sugar of choice through a coffee mill.

Baked Doughnuts

· ·

We have a little secret for you; the magic behind the popular baked cake donuts is simple. They are cake, nothing more. They're just cake batter in a donut pan. The cupcake has taken a new shape, one that we think is really fun. Our recipe is basic with lots of poof and rise. We encourage you to add your favorite toppings, or throw in some chocolate chips to the batter. Need to avoid eggs? Use your favorite egg-free cake recipe here instead.

Yield: One tray (6-8 doughnuts)

DIRECTIONS:

1. Preheat oven to 375 degrees F. Grease doughnut pan.

2. Mix dry ingredients and then whisk in the wet until the batter comes together. Batter will be thick.

3. Pipe or spoon into the doughnut pan. Do not fill more than half of each donut mold full as they will triple in size.

4. Bake 12-14 minutes until lightly golden.

Remove from oven and allow to cool. We recommend dipping these donuts in chocolate glaze. Once cooled, store in a sealed container at room temperature.

Note: For those that do not own a donut pan, use this recipe to make great white cakes or cupcakes, Baking time may need to be extended. Bake until a toothpick comes out clean.

INGREDIENTS:

51 grams potato starch (¼ cup + 1 tablespoon)

36 grams millet flour (¼ packed cup)

65 grams superfine white rice flour (½ packed cup)

½ teaspoon xanthan gum

1½ teaspoons double acting baking powder

½ teaspoon salt

½ cup granulated sugar (any variety)
Note: up to ¾ cup can be used for those that like their doughnuts extra sweet!

1 large egg

2 tablespoons oil or melted butter

105 grams milk (½ cup + 1 tablespoon)

Ask the Expert

Ricki Heller is the genius behind Diet, Dessert and Dogs, a vegan, gluten-free and sugar-free recipe blog. Experimental and creative, Ricki has developed delicious gluten-free baked goods for 10 years. She is the author of four e-cookbooks, including Sweet Freedom.

How long have you been baking gluten-free? I first attempted gluten-free baking about 10 years ago, but that was just for fun and out of curiosity after learning what celiac disease was. I've been baking gluten free exclusively since March 2009.

Do you remember the first thing you ever baked gluten-free (your recipe or someone else's)? How did it turn out? I've always loved quick breads, so the first thing I made was my favorite banana loaf. I simply substituted the same volume of rice flour for the all-purpose wheat flour I'd used before. As you can imagine, I ended up with a banana-scented cement block. I could have used it as a doorstop or a weapon!

What are the top three things every new gluten-free baker should know?
1. Gluten-free baked goods are not the same as wheat-based baked goods. I've changed my outlook from seeking to reproduce wheat-based baking to one that appreciates gluten-free baking on its own merits. These days it can be easy to create gluten-free baked goods that no one will know are gluten-free but that's no longer my goal.

2. Once you embrace gluten-free baking, you will find an enormous range of flavors, textures and types of baked goods that you weren't aware of before. I love the variety of tastes, textures and colors available with gluten-free flours. I know that conventional baked goods would taste to me now.

3. The chemistry of gluten-free baking is different from that of conventional baking so take the time to learn about substitutions, adaptations and which ingredients you need to change or adjust to Yield the results you seek.

Do you have any money saving tips for gluten-free bakers? Buy in bulk when you can. If there's a flour or grain that you use a lot, separate it into smaller bags or containers and store in your fridge or freezer. I've got loads of flours in my freezer! I also buy dried beans instead of canned to use in baked goods in place of bean flours, but always keep two cans of each type of bean in my pantry for days when I am too disorganized to soak beans in advance, or if I think of a new recipe idea on the spur of the moment and don't want to wait. Making your own all-purpose flour mix is a great money saver.

What tips would you give for someone wanting to convert a family favorite recipe

to gluten-free? Begin with the easiest route possible such as an all-purpose, gluten-free flour mix that can be measured in the same quantities as wheat flour. Once you've made it that way, you can experiment by changing up one or two ingredients at a time, and working your way along.

What kind of gluten-free recipes would you suggest for a beginner to start with? Someone else's! Seriously, I wouldn't be too ambitious just starting out.

Is there one recipe that has left you stumped after all these years? Not so much a recipe, but more like all recipes with a particular flour, coconut. I'm still working on recipes that use coconut flour as the main ingredient, and have never been 100% pleased with anything I've come up with. I'll be checking out this book for ideas!

Do you bake by weight or volume? When subbing one flour for another, do you do it by weight or volume? I use both, but more often I use weight, which is more accurate.

What do you generally use as egg replacers in baking? My favorite egg replacer is ground flax seeds mixed with water. A close second is ground chia seeds. I find that flax produces a slightly dryer product, whereas chia tends to absorb and retain more moisture in the final product. And since you can get white chia seeds, they are also better for more delicate desserts that require a lighter look, such as vanilla cakes or cupcakes, for instance.

What kind of dairy free replacements do you like to bake with? I use all the dairy free milks for baking with the exception of hemp milk, which I feel imparts too strong of a flavor to the final baked good. I will use rice milk infrequently even though I love the flavor, because it's so much thinner than the other milks and sometimes doesn't offer enough structure to the baked good.

Is there anything else you think our readers should know about gluten-free baking? In general, gluten-free baking requires more of certain ingredients than wheat-based baking. For example, gluten-free batters and doughs need more liquid than wheat-based ones. In general, cake batters should be thinner and doughs less stiff than raw wheat-based ones to achieve the same results once baked. Second, gluten-free baking needs a bit more leavening than wheat-based baking to rise properly. I always increase the amount of baking powder and/or baking soda slightly in my gluten-free baked goods. Finally, I find that gluten-free recipes often require more spice or seasoning than their wheat-based counterparts. When I bake coffee cake I use nearly double the cinnamon I might add to a wheat-based batter. In general, gluten-free flours are more often whole grain, the assertive flavors of which can otherwise compete with other flavors; adding more spice or flavoring will compensate for that effect.

Chapter 8

Make Your Own Gluten-Free Vegan Muffins & Quick Bread

Gluten-Free/Vegan Quick Bread or Muffin Base

* *

We wanted to develop a recipe for you that is simple, inexpensive and would give you the ability to get creative without the fear of having a flop. Quick bread and muffins were the recipes of choice because this category of baked good is forgiving and can handle some alteration.

INGREDIENTS:

2 cups gluten-free all-purpose flour

1 teaspoon baking powder

1 teaspoon baking soda

½ teaspoon salt

¼-1 tsp xanthan gum

¾ cup granulated sugar

⅓ cup of oil or melted butter

¾ cup milk (dairy or nondairy) + 1 teaspoon vinegar or lemon juice.

1¼ cups of grated fruit/vegetables or fruit/vegetable puree or yogurt/cream cheese/sour cream.

1 teaspoon pure vanilla extract, or any other flavor of extract (optional)

Before we dig in, let's go over some basic tips:

We recommend using full-fat coconut milk from a can for the milk in this recipe. Fat in quick breads/muffins creates a tender, moist texture. If you consume dairy, heavy cream could be an option here too.

There is no risk in overmixing the batter because there is no gluten in this recipe. Isn't that wonderful?! Tough bread and muffins are now a thing of your past.

It is important to get your bread into the oven right after you mix it because the baking soda/powder and vinegar will start reacting once mixed. We want this reaction to happen in the oven, rather than on the kitchen counter in the mixing bowl. So with this being said: make sure to preheat the oven prior to mixing the ingredients and grate/puree/prepare your fruit or vegetable and have it ready prior to mixing as well.

Tips and Substitutions:

The perfect flour/liquid ratio for gluten-free quick bread/muffins is 1:1. In other words, 2 cups of flour in this recipe automatically means that the recipe must also have 2 cups of liquid. The liquid is the first variable that comes in with this recipe. For a part of this recipe's liquid we call for a fruit or vegetable puree OR a finely grated fruit or vegetable. This can include just about anything: mashed bananas, canned pumpkin, sweet potato puree, grated apple, applesauce, canned crushed pineapple. If you don't want your quick bread to be fruit or vegetable based you can use yogurt, sour cream, or cream cheese. (Dairy or non-dairy variations of these will work equally well.)

The sugar used in this recipe must be granulated: Liquid sugars such as honey, coconut syrup, brown rice syrup, and agave add moisture to a recipe. The moisture level in this recipe needs to remain as it is. You can also experiment with the amount of sugar in the recipe. We found ¾ cup to be the perfect amount for banana bread and zucchini bread. Feel free to use more or less granulated sugar than we have based on your own taste.

This recipe should work with any gluten-free all-purpose mix. But the purpose of this book was to teach you how each gluten-free flour works, right? Here's your opportunity to experiment. Provided below is a basic all-purpose mix. Select the flour combination that beckons to you the most. We recommend that you try this recipe a number of times with different flours so you will begin to decipher the taste and textural changes that each of the different flours impart.

ALL-PURPOSE MIX:

¾ cup tapioca or arrowroot starch

¾ cup white rice flour

½ cup flour (Select one: Sorghum, millet, quinoa, garbanzo, teff, or buckwheat flour)

Note: sweet rice flour, coconut flour, amaranth and almond flour are not recommended for this recipe.

Now that you have selected your liquid, granulated sugar and flour mix, it's time to get baking. Here's what you need to make quick bread:

DIRECTIONS:

1. Preheat the oven to 330 degrees F. Grease a loaf pan (9 x 5) and set aside.

2. Prepare grated fruit or veggies or puree.

3. Mix dry ingredients and then add the wet. Mix well. This batter should be fairly thick. Start by using only ¼ teaspoon xanthan gum, adding up to 1 teaspoon if the batter is runny and thin.

4. Feel free to get creative and add additional spices/nuts/seeds/chocolate chips/dried fruit/frozen berries/lemon zest/lime zest/orange zest/fresh chopped herbs.

5. Bake 50-120 minutes. This time will vary based on the ingredients you have selected. You can tell the bread is done by using the toothpick trick.

6. Allow to cool 20-30 minutes before removing from the pan and serving.

Cutting it open too quickly will allow for moisture to escape.

TO MAKE MUFFINS:

1. Divide the batter into greased or lined muffin cups, about ¾ full. Bake at 330 degrees F until they spring back when touched and a toothpick comes out clean.

This bread can be frozen once cooled or store it at room temperature in a sealed bag to prevent drying out.

A Few Flavor Ideas

- **Banana Chai Bread:** Use bananas as fruit puree and then add: 1 teaspoon cinnamon, ½ teaspoon cardamom, ½ teaspoon ground ginger, 1 teaspoon ground cloves and ¼ teaspoon ground pepper. Alternatively, just open and add 1 bag of chai tea to the batter.

- **Pear Walnut Bread:** Use a pear puree and add chopped walnuts and some ground cinnamon.

- **Blueberry Lemon Bread:** Use yogurt/cream cheese/sour cream + frozen blueberries + lemon zest + lemon extract.

- **Banana Bacon Bread:** Use bananas and add cooked crumbled bacon.

- **Peanut Butter Banana Bread:** Use banana as puree and use ⅓ cup peanut butter instead of the oil.

- **Chocolate Chip Zucchini Bread:** Grated zucchini + chocolate chips + 1 teaspoon ground cinnamon.

Chapter 9

Frostings

· ·

2 cups raw cashews, soaked in water 4 hours to overnight

4 dates

½-1 cup full-fat canned coconut milk

¼ cup maple syrup

¼ cup chopped fresh fruit (bananas, blueberries, strawberries, cherries, etc.)

Whipped Cashew Cream

This is a thick frosting, perfect for muffins, hearty cakes, or can even be used as a spread on quick breads.

Yield: 4 cups

DIRECTIONS:
Rinse and drain the cashews. Place in a food processor along with the rest of the ingredients. Start with just ½ cup of coconut milk. Process a few minutes, until completely smooth. Add up to ½ cup more coconut milk if a thinner consistency is desired.

Caramel Cream Frosting

You can adjust this recipe by using more or less powdered sugar. With less, the texture will be closer to a spread that you can use to dip fruit in. If you continue to add powdered sugar, the texture will change to that of a frosting.

Yield: One cup

DIRECTIONS:

1. Start by making your powdered sugar. Place the coconut palm sugar and starch in your blender. Make sure the blender is completely dry inside first. Blend the sugar and starch until it's the consistency of powdered sugar. Once it's ready, set it aside.

2. Rinse and drain the cashews, and puree them in a food processor with the lemon juice, vanilla extract, and salt. Continue to process them until the mixture is a thick, smooth consistency, scraping down the sides as necessary.

3. Add the shortening and process, then add the powdered sugar a little at a time, until you've reached the consistency you like. If a thicker consistency is desired, make more powdered sugar and add slowly.

INGREDIENTS:

1 cup coconut palm sugar (or more as needed)

2 tablespoons tapioca starch or arrowroot starch

1 cup raw cashews, soaked in water 4 hours to overnight

1 teaspoon lemon juice

½ teaspoon pure vanilla extract

¼ teaspoon salt

4 tablespoons shortening

1½ cups fresh berries
(or frozen and
thawed)

1 tablespoon fresh
orange juice

20 drops liquid stevia

Berry Syrup

This is the only recipe in this book using stevia. Although stevia has a bitter aftertaste, it is masked by the sweet berries. Use this as a syrup for your pancakes and waffles or try it drizzled over the Gingerbread Angel Food Cake.

Yield: ¾ cup

DIRECTIONS:

Puree all ingredients in a food processor or blender until smooth. If you're using a berry with large seeds, like raspberries, you can strain the sauce if you prefer not to have them in the syrup.

Homemade Powdered Sugar

INGREDIENTS:

⅓ cup any variety of
granulated sugar

½ teaspoon arrowroot,
cornstarch, tapioca, or
potato starch

All varieties of granulated sugar can become powdered with the use of a blender or coffee grinder. Store bought powdered sugar usually contains cornstarch, which is problematic for some people. For those looking to avoid starch, it can be left out in most cases as its purpose is to help thicken frostings.

Try making powdered sugar out of organic cane sugar, coconut palm sugar, Sucanat, turbinado sugar, or xylitol. Each will provide a different flavor, level of sweetness and may change the color of your frosting slightly. Experiment to find which sugar you like working with best.

DIRECTIONS:

1. Process ingredients in a blender or coffee grinder until light and powdered. Store in an airtight container.

5 tablespoons cold water

1 packet unflavored gelatin

1 cup liquid sweetener (brown rice syrup, agave nectar, coconut nectar, or maple syrup)

Pinch of salt

Marshmallow Creme

Our take is a little healthier and surprisingly easy to make. The different sugars listed as options will create varying levels of sweetness. Select your favorite that best suits your dietary needs.

DIRECTIONS:

1. In a small microwave safe bowl, combine the cold water and gelatin. Microwave for 30 seconds.

2. In a large bowl, combine the gelatin and sugar. Whip vigorously using a mixer 8-10 minutes until it becomes thick. As it sits, it may begin to lose its fluffy appearance and curdle. If this happens you can re-beat with a spoon or spatula briefly. This marshmallow creme will get firm if stored in the fridge.

Note: If you want to keep things extra simple, use Suzanne's Ricemallow Creme, which can be found in many grocery stores.

Dairy-Free Buttercream

Earth Balance Buttery Sticks make flawless buttercream! For those who avoid soy, use their soy-free tub of butter instead. Use this recipe to frost your favorite cake or use a dollop on cookies. This frosting will hold its shape at room temperature.

Note: the amount of powdered sugar needed will range depending on what type of sugar you use. This is especially true when you opt to use our homemade powdered sugar recipe.

DIRECTIONS:

1. Combine softened Earth Balance butter and powdered sugar with a hand mixer.

2. Add more sugar for a thicker frosting; add more Earth Balance butter to thin it out.

Experiment with this frosting to customize the flavor for different applications. Some ideas to get you started:

- **Vanilla:** Add some pure vanilla extract and or fresh vanilla beans.

- **Mint:** Add fresh pureed mint leaves or mint extract.

- **Chocolate Almond:** Add cocoa powder to taste and almond extract.

- **Lemonade:** Add 1-2 tablespoons of condensed lemonade and lemon zest

- **Chai:** Start with ½ teaspoon each of ground cardamom and nutmeg (adding more to taste). Add a dash of pure vanilla extract.

- **Citrus Ginger:** Add 1 teaspoon grated ginger and 1 teaspoon orange or lemon extract.

INGREDIENTS:

2½-3 cups powdered sugar (see powdered sugar recipe)

1 cup (2 sticks) Earth Balance Buttery Sticks or Spread

Basic Coconut Cream Cheese

INGREDIENTS:

1 can full-fat coconut milk (Thai Kitchen brand works best), chilled for at least a few hours

2½ cups coconut flakes (not reduced fat)

¼-½ teaspoon salt to taste

1½-2 tablespoons lemon juice

Liquid sugar to taste (agave nectar, maple syrup, coconut nectar, honey, or liquid stevia to taste)

Dairy-free cream cheese alternatives tend to be comprised of either soy or nuts. We created this version without those two ingredients, as we know that many of you are not able to consume them. This thick cream cheese tastes best at room temperature. If it becomes hard and dry after storing in the fridge, stick it in the microwave 15-20 seconds to soften.

DIRECTIONS:

1. Place can of coconut milk in the fridge for a few hours to chill. This will allow the coconut cream to rise to the top.

2. Using a coffee grinder or powerful blender, make "coconut butter" by processing the coconut flakes until they becomes thick and smooth like peanut butter. You may need to stir the flakes several times until they are fully processed.

3. Place the thick coconut butter in a bowl. Remove can of coconut milk from the fridge and scoop out the thick portion of the heavy coconut cream, which will have risen to the top. Stir it into the coconut butter.

4. Stir in the lemon juice, salt and sugar. Give a taste test and adjust flavoring to taste.

Note: Try adding vanilla or other flavored extracts to this cream cheese. If you would like it thicker, add more "coconut butter". If you would like it thinner, add more coconut milk or liquid sugar.

Coconut Cream Cheese Frosting

. . . .

So close to the real thing, no one will guess it's made without dairy, soy or nuts.

INGREDIENTS:

1 cup coconut flakes (not reduced fat)

1 chilled can of full-fat coconut milk (Thai Kitchen brand is best)

¼ teaspoon salt

½ cup powdered sugar (see powdered sugar recipe)

1½ teaspoons lemon juice

⅛-¼ teaspoon xanthan or guar gum

DIRECTIONS:

1. Using a coffee grinder or powerful blender make "coconut butter" by processing the coconut flakes until they become thick and smooth like peanut butter. You may need to stir the flakes several times until they are fully processed.

2. In a microwave safe bowl, add the coconut butter. Open can of chilled coconut milk and scoop out the heavy cream on top. Mix together and stir in the salt, sugar and lemon juice.

3. Melt mixture in the microwave for 30 seconds to 1 minute. Place in the fridge until thick and chilled.

4. Using a hand mixer, beat in xanthan gum. Start with ⅛ teaspoon, adding only up to ¼ teaspoon total if you want it thicker. Be careful not to add more than this as the frosting can become gummy.

This frosting stores great in the fridge. Use it to top cake or cookies.

Coconut Strawberry "Cream Cheese"

* *

This healthy cream cheese recipe is perfect topped on cake, cupcakes, cookies or a bagel. You'll be surprised how many great uses it has. For variation, try subbing in different varieties of pureed fruit.

Yield: ½ cup

DIRECTIONS:

1. Using a coffee grinder, process the coconut flakes into butter. You may need to stir them several times before they process fully.

2. Next, make your own powdered sugar (or just use store bought). I recommend using a mild tasting sugar like cane or turbinado. Coconut palm sugar has a caramel flavor that may not work best in this application. Xylitol is not recommended.

3. Puree fresh or thawed frozen strawberries.

4. Combine the coconut butter, powdered sugar, strawberry puree, lemon juice, vanilla, and salt. Mix together (this can be done by hand or in a small food processor). At this point, give it a taste test and adjust the ingredients to taste. Store in the fridge.

   Note: If you want the cream cheese thicker, add a pinch (keep it less than ⅛ teaspoon) of xanthan or guar gum or add as many additional coconut flakes ground into "butter" as you want.

Chocolate Glaze

We love using this glaze with our Apricot Brownie Bites, but it can also be drizzled over cookies or cakes. Make sure your ingredients are at room temperature before you start. If not, the glaze will not become as uniformly smooth.

DIRECTIONS:

1. Heat coconut milk in a small pan over low heat. Stir in maple syrup and vanilla extract for a minute.

2. Add chocolate and stir until smooth.

You can dip your baked goods in this glaze and let them cool on parchment paper. Alternatively, you can drizzle the glaze over cookies and cakes.

INGREDIENTS:

(at room temperature)

½ cup full-fat canned coconut milk

6 tablespoons maple syrup

1 teaspoon pure vanilla extract

4 ounces unsweetened chocolate, chopped

3 dried apricots, finely chopped

¼ cup nut or seed
   butter

½ stick (4 tablespoons)
   Earth Balance or
   butter

2-2½ cups powdered
   sugar (see powdered
   sugar recipe)

3 tablespoons milk

Nut or Seed Butter Frosting

Cashew, peanut and sunflower seed butters are our favorites. Different brands of nut butter contain different levels of oil so you may need to adjust this recipe slightly adding more or less powdered sugar and milk to find the results that you like best.

DIRECTIONS:

1. Bring ingredients to room temperature. Combine using a hand mixer. If the frosting beads up, add additional milk ½ teaspoon at a time.

2. Cover and place frosting in fridge until its ready to be used. Try piping this frosting onto jelly-filled cupcakes!

German Chocolate Cake Frosting

* *

This thick frosting is delicious sandwiched between two cookies or spread over a German Chocolate Cake!

DIRECTIONS:

1. Select a base frosting such as Buttercream, Coconut Cream Cheese, or Whipped Cashew Cream.

2. If choosing the Coconut Cream Cheese, omit the lemon juice called for. If choosing the Whipped Cashew Cream, omit the fruit called for.

3. Add vanilla, coconut flakes and nuts.

INGREDIENTS:

1 teaspoon pure vanilla extract

½ cup unsweetened coconut flakes (or more to taste)

½ cup chopped pecans or walnuts (or more to taste)

¾ cup butter, Earth Balance or coconut oil

1¼ cups brown sugar

¼ cup liquid sugar (corn syrup, agave nectar, brown rice syrup, coconut nectar, or honey)

6 ounces canned coconut milk

½ teaspoon salt

1 teaspoon pure vanilla extract

Simple Soft Caramel

. . . .

Our caramel is healthier than the pre-wrapped cubes that you'll find in the candy section of most grocery stores. Pull out your candy thermometer for this one.

DIRECTIONS:

1. In a large heavy-bottomed sauce pan, one large enough to allow for this mixture to expand without overflowing, Combine the butter, granulated and liquid sugar, coconut milk, and salt.

2. Using a candy thermometer, heat the mixture to 248 degrees (firm ball stage). Quickly stir in the vanilla.

3. Pour into a parchment lined 7 x 7 inch square pan, set aside, and allow to cool for several hours until firm. Caramel may also be spooned over cookies, or other favorite desserts while it is still warm. This caramel may be reheated and melted for future use.

Resources

....

Looking for more resources for baking tips and ideas? These are our favorite resources. Some of our ideas have come from cookbooks that aren't gluten-free, so we're including any references that we've found helpful. Check out some of these websites and books. Enjoy!

Books:

Artisanal Gluten-Free Cupcakes by Kelli and Peter Bronski

Beyond the Moon Cookbook by Ginny Callan

Cooking for Isaiah: Gluten-Free and Dairy-Free Recipes for Easy, Delicious Meals by Silvana Nardone

Everyday Raw Desserts by Mathew Kenney

Gluten-Free Baking for Dummies by Dr. Jean McFadden Layton and Linda Larsen

Gluten-Free Makeovers by Beth Hillson

Gluten-Free on a Shoestring by Nicole Hunn

Gluten-Free Quick & Easy by Carol Fenster

Go Dairy Free by Alisa Marie Fleming

Good Morning: Breakfasts without Gluten, Sugar, Eggs or Dairy by Ricki Heller

How Baking Works by Paula Figoni

Kids Can Cook by Dorothy R. Bates

The Flavor Bible: The Essential Guide to Culinary Creativity, Based on the Wisdom of America's Most Imaginative Chefs by Karen Page and Andrew Dornenburg

The Gluten-Free Almond Flour Cookbook by Elana Amsterdam

The Gluten-Free Gourmet: Living Well Without Wheat by Bette Hagman

The Spunky Coconut Cookbook by Kelly Brozyna

Magazines:

Gluten-Free Living
www.glutenfreeliving.com

Easy Eats
www.easyeats.com

Living Without
www.livingwithout.com

Fine Cooking
www.finecooking.com

Blogs and Websites:

Adventures of a Gluten-Free Mom
www.adventuresofaglutenfreemom.com

Affairs of Living
www.affairsofliving.com

Book of Yum
www.bookofyum.com/blog

Celiac Teen
www.celiacteen.com

Chocolate Covered Katie
www.chocolatecoveredkatie.com

Choosing Raw
www.choosingraw.com

Cook it Allergy Free
www.cookitallergyfree.com

Diet, Dessert, and Dogs
www.dietdessertndogs.com

Elana's Pantry
www.elanaspantry.com

Ginger Lemon Girl
www.gingerlemongirl.blogspot.com

Gluten-Free Easily
www.glutenfreeeasily.com

Gluten-Free Gigi
www.glutenfreegigi.com

Gluten-Free Goddess
www.glutenfreegoddess.blogspot.com

Gluten Free on a Shoestring
www.glutenfreeonashoestring.com

Jenn Cuisine
www.jenncuisine.com

Karina's Kitchen
www.glutenfreegoddess.blogspot.com

Pure 2 Raw
www.pure2raw.com

Manifest Vegan
www.manifestvegan.com

She Let Them Eat Cake
www.sheletthemeatcake.com

Silvana's Kitchen
www.silvanaskitchen.com

Simply Sugar & Gluten-Free
www.simplysugarandglutenfree.com

Simply…Gluten-Free
www.simplygluten-free.com

Straight into Bed Cakefree and Dried
www.milkforthemorningcake.blogspot.com

Tasty Eats at Home
www.tastyeatsathome.com

The W.H.O.L.E. Gang
www.thewholegang.org

Whole Life Nutrition Kitchen
www.nourishingmeals.com

The Balanced Platter
www.balancedplatter.com

The Mommy Bowl
www.themommybowl.com

The Spunky Coconut
www.thespunkycoconut.com

Z's Cup of Tea
www.zscupoftea.com

Recipe Index